# SHE RISES LATE AND HER KIDS MAKE HER BREAKFAST

## KERRI POMAROLLI

HARVEST HOUSE PUBLISHERS
EUGENE, OREGON

Cover design by Connie Gabbert Design + Illustration

Front cover photos © CSA-Printstock / iStockphoto ; Jullius / shutterstock

Published in association with the literary agency of WordServe Literary Group, Ltd., www.wordserveliterary.com.

**She Rises Late and Her Kids Make Her Breakfast**

Copyright © 2019 by Kerri Pomarolli
Published by Harvest House Publishers
Eugene, Oregon 97408
www.harvesthousepublishers.com

ISBN 978-0-7369-7750-0 (pbk.)
ISBN 978-0-7369-7751-7 (eBook)

**Printed in the United States of America**

19  20  21  22  23  24  25  26  27  / VP-SK /  10  9  8  7  6  5  4  3  2  1

*To all the readers who think
Nutella should be a food group.*

# BEFORE YOU GET STARTED...

I've been a Christian over 35 years, but some days I feel like my spiritual life is about as mature as my eight-year-old's. Do you ever find yourself paging through magazines and websites, and suddenly the thought occurs to you that you haven't spent any time with God today? Or yesterday? Or, you know...maybe in a long time? And maybe you desire to spend more time with Him, but the hours and days slip away with work deadlines, phone calls, social engagements, children living in your house expecting you to feed them...*every* single day.

This is why I wrote this devotional. I know you only have so much time in the bathroom, and I know that's literally the only time you get to yourself. Some of you try to take a shower alone, but when you look outside the curtain, a tiny human is standing there. She's like a short Norman Bates in *Psycho* demanding to join you. She jumps in with her clothes on, and you let her. You might even call that "bath night." I get it. I live this life day in and day out. This book is for you.

If you are not a mother, this book is for you too. We women all have the same struggles. It's just our circumstances that change. I love God with all my heart, and there are days when I have the luxury and discipline to spend lots of time in His Word. But other days I need something to pick me up and help me start my day. I hope these stories can be a dose of fun and encouragement along with your morning coffee/doughnut/toaster strudel/leftover pizza. (Nobody's judging.)

We all know a daily dose of God's Word is an integral part of any diet, and there is a very real enemy who will do anything to make sure we skip this important nutrient as often as possible. So this book has 60 daily devotionals that I promise will make you laugh, think, and possibly give you a new way to view some things. Most importantly, it will connect you with God's Word. So give me 60 days, and let's see what happens.

Some of you are wondering who the Proverbs 32 Woman in the subtitle of this book is. Is there a chapter 32 in Proverbs you missed? Well, no, but there is a Proverbs 32 Woman, and that's me. And after reading this book, you may realize it's you too.

I've read about the Proverbs 31 Woman for years, and I've always wondered what this woman was really like. Was she even real? I have tried to emulate her, but I don't rise early and I don't plow. I think "gathering food from afar" is referring to Uber Eats! And since I couldn't measure up to the standard she set, I decided I'd embrace my own #hotmess4Jesus life and become a Proverbs 32 Woman instead.

If you are reading this book, you could be one too! Do you think Nutella solves problems? Do you watch the Food Channel and surf Pinterest for recipes that you never—and I mean *never*—make? Do you listen to old songs on the radio and secretly wonder what your boyfriend from high school is up to and then fight the temptation to look him up on Facebook? (And then do it anyway?) God's not mad at you or thinking less of you. He thinks you're delightful and fun and loves every bit of your imperfect self. He didn't create you to be a robot. He created you to embrace this journey through each day He gives you on earth, and He invites you to learn as much as you can about living the best life He intended for you. This life is full of pitfalls, tragedy, tears, and pain, but it's also full of joy, laughter, and incredible moments. We need only to stop long enough to appreciate them.

In this devotional my plan is to explore some of the things the Proverbs 31 Woman can teach us. But I also want us to learn more about God's unconditional, crazy, pure love for every single part of us—the good, the bad, and the unfiltered. I hope you enjoy my stories and see a little of yourself in each one. I just want this book to help women in every life stage. I want to help you realize you are not alone and you are exactly where you are supposed to be. God never intended you to be on the hamster wheel of anxiety, rushing along this path called Modern-Day Womanhood.

The more we read about Him and His heart, the more we can realize that most of our problems are the result of us believing the wrong things about ourselves. Most of us spend more time getting validation from Facebook and Instagram likes than from our heavenly Father. I'm the guiltiest of the bunch. Lately I'm obsessed with Keto recipes and intermittent fasting so I can lose 20 pounds in five days (or so says the Internet).

So for the next 60 days, take a journey with me. We'll see how we all come out at the end.

And if you want to dive deeper into some of these topics, I wrote another book. (Shameless plug: *Confessions of a Proverbs 32 Woman.*) It has, like, real grown-up chapters. Some are maybe even six pages, because I'm deep like that.

Proverbs31Woman@heaven.org

Dear Grace—the Proverbs 31 Woman,

Do you run into a lot of famous people in heaven and try to act natural? Do you know you're fabulous, and a hero? People have been wanting to meet you for centuries.

I hope it's not too much trouble to ask you to read my devotional. I made the chapters short and sweet because we're not in eternity yet and my book is competing with Instagram stories that are only 15 seconds long.

I hope you enjoy my musings. I tried my best to be honest and thoughtful and not sell out my kids too much. I'm the one who will have to pay for their therapy!

I look forward to hearing from you. If you have a phone number, please send it and I will not give it out to anyone...not even my mother. And by the way, if you see Clark Gable, would you let me know? My mom was asking, but I promise that if you say he's there, I won't give your number to her.

And tell Patrick Swayze I said, "Stay golden."

Your friend,
Kerri—the Proverbs 32 Woman

# WHERE DOES THE TIME GO?

*There is a time for everything,*
*and a season for every activity under the heavens.*

**ECCLESIASTES 3:1**

D o you ever feel like the day is half over and you don't even know where it went? I don't know what takes up my time. I get up most mornings with the best of intentions of doing all the important things my adult life requires, and of course adding in something meaningful that's just for me, as the magazines tell me to do. But then life takes over. Suddenly I'm cleaning up after the minions, my daughters Lucy and Ruby, who have infiltrated my house, as well as browsing the Internet for recipes I am never going to make and keeping myself busy with the long list of random activities that really don't bear much fruit. It's a race to the finish line of never-ending tasks, people who need my attention, work obligations, dirty dishes, and jogging in place because I forgot I promised myself I'd work out that day. (Yes, I jog in place, maybe even for three minutes. Then I tell people I worked out. Then I eat pretzels.)

It seems like it was just yesterday that I was 22 years old, fresh out of college, living a life of wild abandon. But you know what? Come to think of it, that's just not true. It's easier to think life was simpler before I had all these responsibilities, but then I remember what those years were like. And they were not easy. When I was 22, I worked three jobs to pay my rent. I might have been more carefree, but I still rushed around like a chicken with my head cut off most days. Circumstances have changed, but I haven't.

I suppose I am a bit more exhausted these days. I try to find an ebb and flow in my schedule, but I haven't even come close to mastering it. And I know in my heart that I'm supposed to enjoy each moment. I've read that message on enough greeting cards. I'm just not very good at doing it. Are you?

The other day I was in a gift store and I saw a plaque that said, "Enjoy the people in your life because they will never be this age again." I thought of my parents in their seventies, and I thought of how I wish they would live forever. I thought of my kids, who seem to be growing at superhero warp speed. I started bawling—yes, *bawling*—in the store. Of course I had to purchase that sign and several other decorative (useless) items.

When I got home that night, I took some time to go through the scrapbooks that my Pinterest-gifted mom had made for me. I saw time passing through the pages of photos and report cards and graduation certificates. I realized the stupid tear-inducing plaque was right. I'd better take in the moments with the people I love, because I'm never going to get them back. The realization hit me hard.

So I called my parents and some old friends just to say hello. (It's a lost art form to make a phone call to a friend for no particular reason.) And the next day I told my kids we were having a "Mommy Lucy Ruby Day." We stayed home from school, ate chocolate chip marshmallow pancakes for breakfast and cheeseburgers for lunch, and watched way too many Hallmark movies. It was perfect. It was bliss. It was just what I needed. I think even they thought it was an awesome day, because Mommy put down her phone and her "work stuff" and just played with them.

I could feel God smiling that day. I had made a point to be grateful for what He's given me. I didn't pester God with all my prayers of worry, stress, and doubt. I simply felt thankful, and I let God know I was grateful for all He has given me. It made us both happy.

Those cheeseburgers and pancakes took a toll, though. Now I'm bloated and full, and I have to go jog in place to burn them off. I may even do four minutes this time! (Nah…who are we kidding? It's winter. I don't need to think about fitness until June!)

. . .

## TO THINK ON

- How have you felt time moving too fast in your life?
- What can you do to slow down and appreciate the moments?

. . .

*Dear Lord,*

*If there were a way to slow down time, I'd pray for You to do it. But I suppose I just need You to help me slow down so I can appreciate all that You've given me in this life.*

*In Jesus' name.*

*Amen.*

# WHAT IT TAKES TO LOOK NATURAL THESE DAYS

*Charm is deceptive, and beauty is fleeting;*
*but a woman who fears the LORD is to be praised.*

**PROVERBS 31:30**

The other day my roommate, Debbie, gave me the sweetest compliment. She said, "You are so naturally beautiful! What's your secret?"

First I was floored by the unexpected flattery. Then I burst out laughing. I don't know what your town is like, but I live in La La Land out here in California, and "natural" beauty is expensive!

A few years ago I saw a picture of myself and was genuinely startled. I realized my hair was highlighted so blonde that I looked like one of the Real Housewives of Orange County. I called my longtime hairdresser and told her I wanted to go au naturel: back to my brunette roots. After about four hours in the salon, I emerged with beautiful brunette locks. Most people seemed to love it. My mother said, "Well, I guess that's the color God gave you, so…" Yes, that's exactly what she said. This woman is 75 years old, and she will die platinum blonde. I bet she's written her hairdresser into her will.

I felt I was making a healthy choice with my hair until about two weeks later when I looked in the mirror and screamed. For the first time in my life there were these gray streaks on the top of my scalp. I pretty much thought I was dying. I had never seen anything like this before. What was this disease on top of my head? WebMD said I would live. But did I want to?

I was back in the salon faster than my kids eat Popsicles. I wasn't going down without a fight. Gray hair may be a natural occurrence in most of the world, but it does not happen in Los Angeles. Could I just accept the sign of the rapidly advancing clock on my head? Or would I fight Mother Nature? Because if that was the case, then game on, Mother! Instead of highlighting my brown roots blonde, I began highlighting my gray roots back to brown.

I've been doing that dance for a couple years now, and recently I stopped to ponder how natural I really am. Let's see...

- For starters, I use self-tanner to make my Irish skin look more Italian. (I'm 25 percent from the Motherland.)

- I discovered Maria, a wonderful neighbor who will come to my home and blow-dry and style my hair, all for much less money than she deserves. Yes, I'm turning into my mother with my weekly hair appointments, and yes, Maria is in my will (on the condition she does my hair in my coffin). And because I work on stage, each hair appointment is a tax write-off.

- I just mortgaged a kidney to get my front teeth veneers extra white, since they were fixed 20 years ago by my friend who was a dental student at the time. It took 13 hours back then, but I think it only cost eight dollars!

- A lady on Facebook asked me if I'd try her eyelash growth product and then write a review on social media, so I've been working on growing my lashes, all so I can show off my new bright-blue mascara from Sephora (my homage to 1989). Speaking of Sephora, not only am I required to wear makeup, now apparently I must contour my cheekbones because the ones I was born with don't look enough like a Kardashian. I also discovered they sell roll-on body glitter, and that has become a daily staple. At my age I must look like a fairy!

- My bathroom is filled with every potion and lotion you've

seen for antiaging, and this is because my mom is obsessed with QVC and she sends me her leftovers.

- My bras are about as padded as the ones I wore in eighth grade, even after two kids.

- My friends Susie and Claire come over to my house and tell me how to match my outfits, because even though I am a grown-up, it appears I don't know how to appropriately dress myself for public consumption.

- I own a Pilates machine that is sitting in my backyard. I bought it off Craigslist because every good woman in LA is required to do a minimum number of hours of Pilates every week. (I meet my quota in my knock-off Lululemon pants...from Goodwill.)

- My toes are painted in various colors and polka dots because my eight-year-old thought that would look cool.

So, come to think about it, from my head to my toes, there is very little natural about me. Does this make me feel guilty? Okay, okay... now that I've written it down, it's food for thought. I'm a modern-day Christian woman, and it takes a village for me to look oh-so-natural in those oh-so-filtered "nonfiltered" Instagram shots I post every day. But what would I change?

And here's another question: Is God okay with all of this? Didn't the ladies in the Bible get piercings and tattoos? And didn't they partake in some intense mud baths? I wonder what kind of beauty rituals the Proverbs 31 Woman had. The Bible says she rose early, but I bet that was the only time she could get a bath before her kids got up.

Now, I have two daughters, and the little one, Ruby, often comes in my bathroom and says, "Mommy, I want lipstick just like you." So I let her wear some, and yes, she shows up at Sunday school looking a bit like a painted lady at times.

I have a verse plastered on my bathroom wall where I can see it every day. It's from Psalm 46:5: "God is within her, she will not fall." When I saw it again this morning, I burst out laughing. Those words are posted above all of my makeup and serums that I include as part of my so-called "natural" beauty routine. Oh, the irony.

The question I ponder is this: How important is all of this beauty nonsense to me? Could I live without it? The answer is yes, of course I could. Do I want to? Not really. Is God telling me it's all right to play dress up once in a while? I think He's okay with it, as long as the most important part of me is untainted: my heart. Underneath the glitter and frosting, what is going on with me on the inside? Where do I find my real value? I'd like to tell you I find my value in my faith in God, and I'm working to make sure that's a true statement.

But come on, even God likes a little glitter.

(And by the way—the Pilates machine has never been used. It's back on Craigslist if you want to buy it.)

• • •

## TO THINK ON

- What's your beauty routine like for your heart and mind?
- What are you doing to nurture it?
- What "beauty tip" might God give you right now?

• • •

*Dear God,*

*Help me remember that I am a one-of-a-kind original. You only make masterpieces. Help me see myself the way You do.*

*In Jesus' name.*

*Amen.*

Day 3

# STOP IT!

*Have I not commanded you? Be strong and courageous.*
*Do not be afraid; do not be discouraged,*
*for the LORD your God will be with you wherever you go.*

**JOSHUA 1:9**

My older daughter, Lucy, got up early this morning and came into my bed as she sometimes does. "I'm not tired, Mom," she declared. "I don't want to go back to sleep." I wrapped her whole body tightly in a mom cuddle-grip, and soon enough, she was back in dreamland.

I prayed over her and held her. I saw how beautiful and peaceful she looked, and I wanted to scream at the top of my lungs, "Stop it! Just stop it! All of it! Stop growing older. Stop inching closer to the day you won't be here anymore. Stop growing up in this scary world where you will be faced with questions I don't want you to have to answer. And for goodness' sake, stay the age you are today because people tell me raising a teenager is about as bad as walking on hot coals! Please just stay right here and help me stop time. I want it to stay like this forever!"

I hate change. I really do. I even fear it at times. And that's ironic, because I've made my career in a business where nothing is stable, and I'm in a new city with new people every week. So much of my life is uncertain. I just wish some things could stay the same. Now, I don't wish my kids were babies again. I hated diaper changes and breastfeeding. But I'd like to keep them where they are right now. People keep telling me lovely things like, "Enjoy it while it lasts, because the teenage years are coming!" They make teens sound like the Loch Ness monster! Please tell me that's not true.

There is so much I want to protect my kids from, and I know I won't be able to. Lucy got her first Kindle yesterday, and if she wants to, she can get on the internet when I'm not around. I can make rules, but sometimes rules are broken. What will happen when she sees something accidentally or on purpose that can hurt her and I'm not there to stop it? What happens when the world tells her lies about herself and she believes them? I'm not prepared for any of this, and I'm scared. Just for today I wish I could cuddle with my daughter and stroke her head and have her be my baby.

I wonder if this is how God feels about us. He's known us from the moment we were created, and He watches us grow up and run and jump and make mistakes that break His heart. He doesn't want to see us get hurt, just like I don't want to see my daughters get hurt. But God created us with free will. He didn't want to create puppets or robots. He wanted children who love Him because they choose to, who make good choices because they choose to. He could easily sweep in right now and solve all the world's problems, and I don't know why He hasn't rescued us from all of the enemy's snares. But I can be confident that He is watching over us. He is equipping us with His Word and His Holy Spirit to keep fighting all the battles. We know who wins the war.

Lucy is fierce. She was asked to dress like a maiden or princess for her horse camp party, and she came out in full battle regalia. She wore a black wig and shouted, "I'm Joan of Arc!" Last fall she decided she wanted to play football, so she did. She was the only girl in the whole league. I'm glad my daughter is fierce. I'm glad she was raised to know she is powerful and strong.

Most of all, I'm glad she has faith in a God who is real to her. She knows she can talk to Him. I can't fight all her battles for her, like the time a certain girl was mean to her at school (although I thought about having some words with that kid!). I just have to continue to do my best to have a good relationship with her so that when she is in need, she knows she can come to me and when she screws up, she won't be afraid to talk to me about it. That is what God is asking of me. He wants me to come to Him in all circumstances. Just the way my kids crawl into my arms when they need me.

• • •

## TO THINK ON

- How do you feel about change? Is it something scary or something to embrace?
- Is there an area in your life where you wish you could stop time? Why?
- How can we let God help us embrace change in our lives?

• • •

*Dear God,*

*I don't like change, and sometimes it even scares me.*

*I know I can only get through life's changes by depending on You for peace and guidance. Please help me know You have my life mapped out before me, and then the twists and turns will be no surprise. Jesus, please take the wheel!*

*In Jesus' name.*

*Amen.*

# I HOPE THERE AREN'T DISHES IN HEAVEN

*But all things should be done decently and in order.*

**1 CORINTHIANS 14:40 ESV**

really think there is something wrong with me. I can't even blame my mother for this one. But when I walk in my house, no matter where I've been or what time it is, I compulsively feel the need to clean or straighten up. It's like a sickness or something.

I remember being away for a life-changing weekend of ministry. Jesus moved mountains. I felt refreshed, renewed, and enlightened. The Holy Spirit touched me, and I knew things were going to be better and different from now on. And then I got home.

My house looked like it had been robbed and nobody took anything! Somehow I felt as though all Jesus had done over the weekend suddenly disappeared into the dust-filled air. I gave polite greetings to my children, and without even knowing it, I began straightening tennis shoes and blankets. I was muttering under my breath, "Why am I the only one who believes dishes go *in the sink?*"

Nice role model, Kerri. I thought of all those thousands of people to whom I had just preached the gospel about peace and laughter. I wondered if they would love to see me now, up to my ears in Lysol wipes, throwing out pizza boxes with strands of mozzarella still attached—and considering if I should grab and eat one of the pepperoni slices—as I grumbled and complained.

The work is never, ever done. And I know what you're thinking:

*She must have OCD.* That would make sense, but I'm not obsessively compulsive. I don't have to clean every single crumb off the floor, and everything doesn't have to be perfect. I just constantly feel the need to straighten up. I feel compelled to make sure every dish is soaking, drying, or in the dishwasher.

To make matters worse, I kind of have this ghetto dishwasher. It kind of works, but not really. I'm a renter in the house I live in, and I've learned this: the less I bother my landlord, the less she thinks about raising my rent. So I can keep my mouth shut about the dishwasher situation. But as I was washing my hundredth cup today, I thought, *I really hope there are no dishes in heaven.*

Now, I don't mean to say I don't want heaven's food. When I picture heaven, I see scrumptious, mouthwatering buffets with no lines. I imagine food that has no calories. I'm just hoping the plates we eat on—that are made of gold, obviously—instantly evaporate into thin air. Like the buffets in Las Vegas, I hope we can get a clean plate as many times as we want.

Okay, don't make fun of me. I've actually come up with some strategies to solve this problem with a tiny bit of success. If you know me, you know one of my favorite places on earth is the Dollar Store. Truly, I find great joy and satisfaction from spending $23.99 at the Dollar Store, knowing I got $455.00 worth of groceries. Yes, I buy fruit there. Don't judge me. Grapes are seven dollars per pound at Ralphs Grocery. At the dollar store? Three pounds are a dollar, baby. I'm fully aware that those grapes did not come from Italy, and the country they did come from might be harboring diseases. But then again, we all have to die someday. I'm thankful that God invented fruit rinse, since my kids eat about 13 pounds of frozen grapes every week. I've convinced them that frozen fruit is like Popsicles—it's a special treat!

A couple months ago I was shopping in the party aisle at the Dollar Store, and I saw these really cute plates with emoji characters on them. Normally I would be buying these for some party we were hosting, but they were selling 20 plates for one dollar. I did the math and justified that buying these plates would actually be a good investment, and even good for the environment. I could use them in my kitchen daily, and I could save on all the water and dish soap. I realize we need to save trees, but since they were already made and printed, it's not like I killed the trees. You see my logic, right?

Oh, and on a side note, that day while I was shopping, I noticed a nice-looking gentleman giving me quite a few smiles. Then he sort of followed me from aisle to aisle, and he tried to make pleasant conversation. I know I'm old, but I do believe this man was hitting on me. My response in my head was, *Are you kidding me? I know you're good-looking, but there is no way I'm going out with a man who shops at the Dollar Store!* Now, I realize I was shopping there, but there is only room in any relationship for one of us to be poor enough to shop at the Dollar Store!

If he had been at the BMW dealership, making conversation with me as I was walking by, perhaps I'd have been more open. But a girl today has to have some strict rules. And I've learned my lesson from that time when I made the decision to marry for *love*, dumb as it was. I married a comedian with no car. I've decided if I ever get married again, I'll marry for old money. It's easier.

All the single women reading this are horrified right now, and all the married women are wanting to give me a high five! They never tell you this stuff in premarital counseling.

Okay, so I bought the emoji plates. True, they aren't as sturdy as real plates, but they have cut down on the amount of dishwashing by about 3 percent. Is this enough to make a difference? Unfortunately, no. I'm still constantly washing, scrubbing, or soaking dishes. But I tried! That hasn't stopped me from buying paper plates; it gives me some sense that I'm saving myself some time. What would Dave Ramsey think? He'd probably think the whole idea wasn't smart. But I don't care. Today I'm sick of washing dishes. I'm also done with picking up socks and straightening pillows.

They say a mother's work is never done, and I believe it. But whose fault is that? Ours! I can't walk by my stove without wiping it down if I see a smudge of leftover spaghetti sauce. I have to make sure my Keurig machine is fully stocked and the Stevia packets are lined up. Could I learn to be happy if my kitchen was a little messier? Would the world end if I waited to clean the peanut butter off the counter until later in the day? Am I even capable of that kind of change? There are certainly millions of people out there living blissfully happy lives with peanut-butter-stained counters and clothes all over the bedroom floor. Should I try to be more like them? Are they happier? They sort of seem happier. A bunch of stuff that bothers me doesn't seem to bother them.

But here I go again, comparing myself to other people…millions of other people I don't even know! I'm just not sure what to do about this behavior in my life. I could narrow it down to cleaning, but we all know it's not about that. It's never *just* about the cleaning. I've been in enough counseling sessions to know that. But what is it about? Why can't I just relax about certain things? Will there be maid service in my mansion in heaven, or will I be asking Saint Peter if they have Lysol? I mean, the streets are paved with gold, but who sweeps them? It's probably going to be me! "Oh Lord, cure me of this compulsion. Get me off the hamster wheel of comparisons. I know You want me to enjoy my time here on earth and I'm missing the joy of living obsessing over these tiny details."

If you resonate with this type of behavior, try to take a step back the next time you realize you're doing it. Ask yourself, "Is this where I really want to be right now? Where is the best use of my time?" And see what you hear.

• • •

## TO THINK ON

- If you're not opposed to washing dishes, is there a different never-ending task that seems to distract you from being in the moment?

- What can you do to stop it from being such a distraction?

• • •

*Dear God,*

*Help me find my balance and focus on what You deem important. Help me realize when I'm out of sorts. Bring me back to a place of peace.*

*In Jesus' name.*

*Amen.*

# HOW DOES MY GARDEN GROW?

*I am the true vine, and my Father is the gardener. He cuts off every branch in me that bears no fruit, while every branch that does bear fruit he prunes so that it will be even more fruitful.*

**JOHN 15:1-2**

f you came to my house and pulled up in my driveway, you might say, "Wow, Kerri, what a green thumb you must have. Your garden is lovely." I would politely thank you, and I would shamelessly take all the credit for the beautiful flowers all over my yard that I so painstakingly planted.

And by I *planted*, I mean that I've chosen the flowers, and two very charming gardeners named Ciro and Juan have put them in the ground for me. Then I give them money. It's taken four years to achieve this vision I had of a wild English garden, but the labor has finally paid off.

I do all the watering, and that counts for something, right? I keep the plants and flowers alive. And I love my flowers so very much. I even have a lime tree, a mandarin orange tree, some radishes, and a tiny avocado plant. In 14 years, we'll have avocados!

Last summer I was a bit overly ambitious. I must have accidentally been on Pinterest, because I decided to plant all these herb pots so I could be Martha Stewart with my fresh sage, mint, and oregano. I planted each in their individual pots and I did what the instructions said, but nothing happened. (You know how the *H* is silent in the word *herb*? Well, all of my actual herbs were silent.) Let's just say my herbs will continue to arrive in those little round containers I get at the grocery store. Oh well, you can't win 'em all!

I relish taking care of my garden, and it's something I look forward to every day. I love getting out in my yard with the hose, watering every single root. There was a time when California was in a drought, so I wasn't able to water my plants for a while. Everyone was encouraged to do drought-tolerant landscaping, and let me tell you, it was ugly. I like colors, and I'm committed to taking good care of my daisies and sunflowers and lavender plants.

Anyway, every morning I go outside to make sure that each one, big and small, gets plenty of water. I feel great joy when I come out the next day to see them growing bigger and taller, into more colorful creations. I think this is one of simplest things that brings me the most joy. I just add water, and these beauties do their thing. Why can't cooking be that easy? Trust me, I've tried those box recipes that say, "Just add water." It's not that simple, and maybe I really shouldn't be buying lasagna from the Dollar Store, but that's for another day. Back to my horticulture routine.

It's not uncommon for me to stand out there 20 to 30 minutes, sometimes pruning brown leaves and watering my garden and my grass. If the grass gets any brown spots, I'm on top of it right away with my trusty hose to make sure the grass will be green in no time.

This morning, as I was standing in my driveway, admiring my pink bougainvillea, it occurred to me that this daily routine is effortless and joyful. And it's almost like God spoke to me, saying, "This is how I feel about My children." God tends to every single one of His children, far and wide, without fail. He never misses a branch, leaf, or root. He knows our every move, need, hope, and dream. He keeps a watchful eye on the ones who are ill, and He does what He can to nurse them back to health.

You could say the weeds and bugs are like Satan and the snares of this world. They are here to kill and destroy and wreak havoc on God's creation. But God, as the constant gardener, is there with water, fertilizer, or sometimes a gentle pruning, all to bring us back to a life where we can grow and thrive.

I can look back on the times in my life where it seems the dry, brown patches far outnumbered the healthy, green spots. Somehow God got me out of those seasons, and it took a lot of pruning. Sometimes He used some light garden shears, and other times I'm sure He needed a pickax! Sometimes He was pruning a relationship, a job, a situation I had put myself in that was only causing harm. In a lot of those seasons, I was young, and I had no idea it was God at work behind the scenes. I just thought people were leaving me, or life was changing beyond my control. It wasn't easy, and it hurt at times. I have been known to be a bit stubborn. But I can't even imagine where I'd be if God hadn't rescued me from a life with weeds. Anyway, the bottom line is this: "Thank You, Jesus, for delivering me from evil."

• • •

## TO THINK ON

- Can you think of times in your life where God had to prune things, or even people?

- Did you know it was happening? If you did, did you know it was God?

- Is there anything in your life right now that could use a good pruning?

• • •

*Dear God,*

*If there are brown spots in my life that need to be pruned, I give You permission to remove them. Please be gentle. Thank You for taking the time to care for me daily and attend to my needs. Thank You for knowing how to help me grow and thrive, even when it hurts.*

*In Jesus' name.*

*Amen.*

Day 6

# BLAME IT ON THE RAIN

*The thief comes only to steal and kill and destroy; I have*
*come that they may have life, and have it to the full.*

**JOHN 10:10**

The first night of our vacation started with a gigantic fight with Lucy because she ratted me out to my mother. She told my mom that I had taken her to buy new clothing because I had somehow lost all the clothing Grandma had purchased for her over the past six months. Then I was trying to give Ruby a bath, which ended up being an hour-long incident and resulted in something that looked like a crime scene. I proceeded to get ready for bed, applying Icy Hot to my aching neck, and then made sure everything was put away in our vacation rental.

Speaking of my aching neck, I had to go out to the truck to get my neck massager. I could feel the raindrops as I walked barefoot out into the parking lot on the pavement. And immediately I was transported back to a moment sometime in my twenties somewhere in Pennsylvania, a summer night like this…an apartment where I was living… There was a boy, there was a date, and there was a good-night kiss that seemed to last forever and there was rain…lots of rain. No, this wasn't a Hallmark movie; things like this actually happened once or twice in my former life a long time ago.

Yes, all the clichés were wrapped up in one moment where time stood still: we kissed in the summer rain…he was dreamy…and that's pretty much all I remember clearly. It's not like he was one of the great loves of my life or that this was some moment I've replayed a thousand times in my head. It's just that tonight this memory that had been tucked away in the back of my mind for so many years came rushing back. I felt the rain on my forehead, and I remembered what it was like to have someone kiss me in the rain, and it was sweet.

I'm a single mom of two beautiful daughters. Most of my days are centered around work and worrying about my aging parents and trying to be a good mom and making sure my kids don't look homeless when they show up for school and that there's at least one vegetable on their plates weekly. I never wanted to be a divorced woman. When I said, "I do," I thought I was saying those words to somebody who would want to hold me forever and have more moments that were joyful than those that would cause much sadness. I wanted to be in a marriage where we would hold hands and walk in the rain when we were very old, but alas, my story has not ended that way. Life has a way of being more like a Lifetime movie than a Hallmark movie sometimes.

And I suppose that's okay. I'm grateful for the rom-com moments I've had along the way that made me feel alive. I think when we're young and invincible and the world is ours to conquer, we don't stop and savor the great, the tragic, and the magical moments that happen to us. I don't have photos of all my great moments for all the world to see. But I have memories and images that are ingrained into my mind and they sometimes make unplanned appearances and cause all the "feels" to occur in the most delightful way. I'm not dying to contact that boy, although we all know it wouldn't be that hard to do. He's actually somewhere on my friends list on Facebook, I believe.

I don't want to believe all the movie magic moments are over. I may be a bit older and wiser, but I'm not emotionally dead. I just tucked that part of my life away for a while because divorce was so hard and it was beyond my imagination to hope for a second chance. It's been more than several years now, and I always tell people, "I don't need love; I have Netflix." But I don't want to become one of those people who sit at home (or in my case, lie in bed under my amazing Pottery Barn duvet) and watch other people's life moments without experiencing some greatness of my own. I'm not done with love.

Too many of us are caught up in the rat race of our own existence, coming home and numbing ourselves out with our vice of choice: food, TV, social media. We're stressed out during the day, and when we zone out as we scroll through other people's experiences, we don't even consider the fact that we're not really living. And I'm talking to myself here. I'm not saying I need to go join eHarmony to make my life meaningful or FarmersOnly (come on, you thought about it!).

I don't think tonight was a coincidence. I believe it was actually God reminding me I was made to love and be loved. And it's okay to hope again for that to come into my life. But even if it doesn't come in a romantic way, I have love all around me. I have these crazy kids who cuddle with me and watch Food Network. I have women in my life who will gather at my home for food and prayer. I have a brother and mom and dad who are still on this earth. We take road trips and celebrate holidays and eat processed foods that will clog our arteries and enjoy some pretty insane and fun times together. I have friends from past and present spread out all over the country who come in and out of my life. I might not get to see them in person or talk to them on the phone that often, but they helped shape who I am and no amount of time or distance can change that kind of love. (And who else can I call and sing Journey to at full blast when their songs come on the radio? Thanks, Tracey!)

Anyone who knows me knows I was always the most hopeful romantic. If you don't believe me, I wrote an entire book about it! And the devil has a way of attacking what is dearest to us and making us feel like we screwed up so badly we will never get that precious thing back. But he's a liar, and God never said that. God never ever told me I was going to have a life without love or magical moments. If they stopped happening it's because I stopped seeing them. My life may not be worthy of a Sandra Bullock screenplay, but I get to spend tomorrow swimming with my two kids, eating cheese puffs and Lucky Charms, and having homemade barbecue for dinner with peach cobbler and watching a Gene Kelly movie with my parents and my kids. If that's not love, I don't know what is.

As a side note: If either of my daughters happen to be reading this someday, I still stand by my rule: all your kisses will be saved for your wedding day, and even then you have the right to wait. Mommy loves you. Now go watch the Christian Movie Channel.

• • •

## TO THINK ON

- Have you had any raindrop moments that brought you back to another place in time?
- How did they make you feel?
- Is there a part of your life you tucked away seemingly forever?
- If there is, who told you it was gone with no return?

• • •

*Dear God,*

*Help me remember You are the God who created us to feel so many things. Help me see when the enemy is telling me a lie about my life. You are a God who believes in second chances. Show me how to hope again.*

*In Jesus' name.*

*Amen.*

# MY PARENTS' HOUSE IS A DEN OF SIN

*Do you not know that your bodies are temples of the
Holy Spirit, who is in you, whom you have received
from God? You are not your own; you were bought at
a price. Therefore honor God with your bodies.*

**1 CORINTHIANS 6:19-20**

know this may be shocking, but my parents are drug dealers. No, they aren't into crack, cocaine, or meth. But their drug of choice is just as addictive, and when I walk into their house I am powerless to resist the smells, the feasts for my eyes…the *sugar*! That's right, my parents have been pushing sugar on me since the day I was born (no, scratch that, since the day I was conceived). I was a Coke baby. My mom drank Coca-Cola like it was going out of style when she was pregnant with me, and it is still flowing abundantly in their home.

Yes, I became addicted to "the devil's juice" from my youth, and it's not my fault. If you were a child of the 1980s, you know no one cared about nutrition. I was awakened every day with a little sugar pill called a Flintstones vitamin and enjoyed my breakfast of Fruity Pebbles or Lucky Charms cereal with milk from a cow. That's right, we drank milk from a cow and water from the tap! I know, that explains a lot about my generation. Some of you even drank water from a hose!

When I was kid, we carried our lunch in a Snoopy lunch box and had a white bread ham sandwich with no crust, Cheetos, and a Twinkie for lunch, and a Hostess cupcake for a snack. My teachers thought I had attention deficit disorder. Now I look back and think they should have blamed my lunch.

So I grew up eating sugar like it was a food group. Later I ignored all the warnings that it was not a wise decision to eat salt-and-vinegar potato chips and Coke for dinner like my dad did every night. I existed on banana splits, soda, boxed cereal, and candy for most of my life. I moved to the land of fruits and nuts (California) and still never changed my ways because we all know Nutella makes your problems go away. And the fact that I spent most of my life as a size 4 gave me all the freedom to gorge my little heart out.

Fast-forward several years and jean sizes, and I came to the cold, hard realization that I cannot go on eating like a college freshman with absolutely no consequences. We could talk about health issues, but who are we kidding? I'm talking about not wanting to be the funny *and* chubby friend of my group in LA. I had to double down on some serious life choices, and I've done okay. I just had to face the reality that Kit Kats and ice cream and I can only have a relationship outside of my own home. That goes for cookies, cakes, and anything involving the word *chips*. I cannot have them in my house. I ate so much of my kids' Halloween candy that I literally handed Ruby her candy and said, "Hide this from Mommy. I trust you more than I trust me!"

This week I flew to the great state of Georgia and entered my parents' "den of sin" with great intentions and willpower. Before we even got home, my dad insisted we stop at Popeye's for a little healthy dinner drive-through. I was greeted in their home with all sorts of seasonal Easter candy bowls. No matter what holiday it is, my mother has bowls full of seasonal wrapped candy. Her mother did the same, but my grandma had a coffee table glass bowl with that hard-striped candy that had never been touched since the Civil War. Anyone remember that?

I made it through my first couple hours only caving to a few chocolate mints and some form of corn syrup juice product that resembled lemonade. I didn't pop open the Cokes until after dinner, and it was only "just a sip" about hundred times until the first bottle was gone. I hit rock bottom when my daughter asked me to watch a movie and she came out with a huge bowl of cheese puffs. Like my dad always says, "The first one's free." It was downhill from there.

They have this cavernous room they call a pantry; I call it Temptation Island. My parents are the people who still buy Krispy Kreme doughnuts, candy, chips, and gigantic marshmallows (not to put in hot cocoa; just to eat and clog their arteries). I brought health food with me and put it on the shelf next to the yellow marshmallow bunnies and Kit Kats and Almond Joy candy bars. But the doughnuts were whispering my name. I ate three Krispy Kreme doughnuts, then hid the bag. Except I knew where I hid the bag, so I went back behind the potatoes and ate two more.

After we all watched a movie together, I went to the devil's playground (pantry) all alone and ate Lucky Charms out of the box like a crack addict. I knew this was bad behavior as I washed it down with Coke, so I stopped and walked away. But as the taste of sugary sweetness and chemicals started to fade from my mouth, I waded back into the pantry and ate four more servings of Lucky Charms and peanut butter crackers and then, just to seal the deal, I ended it with Kit Kats… (yes, plural).

I'm a grown woman, and apparently I have no willpower against my own addictions. Yes, I am a sugar addict, and no amount of jogging in place is going to make up for Binge-Fest 2018 that happened today.

I know the Bible says gluttony is a sin, but I have not done a lot of research on what qualifies as gluttony. I had 30 minutes of gluttony today and, out of 24 hours, that isn't so bad, is it?

I know that a lot of people have serious problems with food. Joking aside, it is important to examine our lives and see if, in times of stress, there is anything (such as food) that is becoming more of a comfort to us than God. If so, then it's time to pray to God and ask Him where the root of that need is coming from. When I get bad news, a piece of chocolate cake is sometimes the first thing I reach for. That's probably not the best choice, and I can admit that. The apostle Paul wrote in 1 Corinthians 10:31: "So whether you eat or drink or whatever you do, do it all for the glory of God."

Just because we're not doing illegal things doesn't mean we don't have idols. Maybe it's time to take a look at your life and dare to ask God to reveal to you any idols or crutches that you turn to instead of Him. I know it's scary, but be brave. It's worth it in the long run. And hey, you might end up healthier and better off in the end.

• • •

## TO THINK ON

- What is your relationship with food? In good times and bad, do you turn to food first?
- If you use food as a comfort or coping mechanism, ask God to reveal to you when that started.
- Ask God to help you realize the next time you are turning to food instead of to Him and see if there is another way to handle those emotions.
- Remember, prayer has no calories!

• • •

*Dear God,*

*I know the world is full of temptations and You promised You wouldn't allow me to be tempted more than I can handle. Please help me find moderation and self-control when I am tempted, especially when it comes to my sweet tooth.*

*In Jesus' name.*

*Amen.*

# I HAD TO BREAK UP WITH MY EX-BOYFRIENDS

*For you were called to freedom, brothers. Only do*
*not use your freedom as an opportunity for the*
*flesh, but through love serve one another.*

**GALATIANS 5:13 ESV**

You can say I'm weird, but I've generally made a habit of keeping in touch with most of the guys I dated. I even wrote a book about them. I didn't have angry partings, so it seemed only natural to stay friends.

When I was growing up and my heart was broken by Bachelor #3, I liked being able to call Bachelor #2 and have him tell me I was pretty and he still loved me. It was always good to have backups, and it was totally innocent. As we all got older and have kept in touch, I've gotten to know some of their wives and children through the years with travel from my job and the occasional check-in phone call.

I was always respectful when talking to any of my exes and kept the conversation aboveboard and about work, family, etc. We never got too deep. But occasionally I had to steer a phone conversation with an ex or two in the right direction if they wanted to discuss any marital problems or got a bit too nostalgic or flirty. I was 100 percent transparent in my marriage. My ex-husband knew about every phone call and conversation. He liked to joke that in any given city he was subjected to having dinner with someone his wife had dated.

Anyway, when I was going through my divorce, my emotions were painfully raw. I was losing my best friend. I talked to supportive exes who told me I was pretty and made me feel special. But something had changed, and it didn't feel okay anymore. I was now a single woman talking to married men. Even if they were old friends, it didn't feel right. I didn't say anything wrong, but I was going through a very insecure time in my life, and I found myself caring a little too much if they "liked" my latest Facebook post. That was a clear red flag that I needed to make a change. I knew that, to protect my heart and mind, I needed to break up with my exes. I didn't make a big deal about it; I just took their phone numbers out of my cell. That way it wouldn't be easy to text or pick up the phone for a quick affirmation.

When you have a shared romantic past with someone, it's difficult not to idealize that relationship. Marriage can be tough, and the devil is really sneaky at blurring old memories, making the past seem much more appealing. In times of emotional turmoil, we can be especially vulnerable to falling into a trap from Satan. We may think we're immune, but we're not…not at all.

I can't count the number of stories I've heard of extramarital affairs starting with a few innocent conversations at work or emails or messages over social media. It's no joke. We have to protect ourselves with whatever means necessary and get our heads right with God.

Being the pack rat and incredibly sentimental person I am, I have kept a lot of old memories in my garage. Just one photo can transport me back to a moment in time, and all those warm and fuzzy feelings can resurface. Trust me: I have Sirius radio, and one of my favorite stations plays '80s music. The minute Bon Jovi comes on, I'm pulling over, crying, thinking about an ex-boyfriend and prom and my pink corsage. Then the temptation comes to reach out in that moment of emotion and share my mental breakdown/memories.

Our minds are powerful things. Married or single, we must respect the healthy boundaries God created with our male relationships for our own good. In the words of Princess Elsa, "Let it go…!" I still have guys in my life whom I call dear friends, but 99 percent of the time, if we are hanging out, they are playing more with my kids than talking to me, and I end up becoming better friends with their wives, some of whom I introduced them to. I think male/female friendships can be awesome, but I always want to be sure I'm staying in my lane for my own heart's sake. God doesn't want to see me get crushed in a sinful and painful situation. And that, my friend, is why I am in a committed relationship with Netflix. It's so fulfilling, and we don't have any jealousy (unless I cheat on Netflix with Amazon Prime).

• • •

## TO THINK ON

- Just between us, are there any male relationships that take up a little too much of your thought life? What about in the past?
- Did you pray through it and get your thought life right with God?
- Do you need to make any adjustments in your dealings with any men right now? God's not mad at you if anything is out of line. Just take this opportunity to think it through and make the necessary changes.

• • •

*Dear God,*

*Thank You for creating men and women differently. I know I can have healthy relationships with friends of the opposite sex, but please always help me to be respectful of the boundaries You set up for me. If there are any relationships in my life right now that are a little off-kilter, show me how to make the necessary adjustments for my own good.*

*In Jesus' name.*

*Amen.*

# I LOVE IT WHEN THEY CRY

## Truth in Parenting

*Then they cried out to the LORD in their trouble,*
*and he delivered them from their distress.*

**PSALM 107:6 ESV**

Okay, here is something I think a lot of moms think but are afraid to say out loud: I secretly love it when my kids are hurting.

I'm not talking about anything major but, you know, the regular kind of pain that happens when you are under the age of 12 and you trip over your sister's Barbie doll or scratch your back jumping off the ottoman onto the wood floor or get your feelings hurt because your sister ate the last cookie.

I have two kids who pretty much think they are invincible. They both came out of the womb that way. Lucy thinks she can fly, and she's been literally trying to walk on water like Peter by jumping in the bathtub since she was three. She'd repeat, "I have the faith! I can do this!"

But from a very young age, both of these independent little minions have pretty much set sail on their own course. I didn't have "cuddly" kids, unless they wanted to do something with me, such as watching *The Golden Girls* past their bedtime. And they are both little drama queens in their own way. For example, Ruby had a playdate with her friend Mikaila, who had her leg in a cast. The next morning Ruby said she had mysteriously injured that same leg. She claimed she could not walk, and she requested crutches and had to be carried around the house. Lucy had a sore throat, and she told everyone at her school she had scarlet fever, just like Laura Ingalls from *Little House on the Prairie*. I have no idea where they got it from!

But this week we were visiting my parents in Georgia, and they had a big storm with thunder and lightning. My California kids have barely ever seen rain, much less lightning. I was in another room when all of a sudden these kids were yelling at the top of their lungs, "Mommy! Mommy! Help! We're scared." Lucy started packing rations for the possible power outage. She was grabbing flashlights and power bars, and she kept insisting we stay in the basement and away from all windows. She must have seen this in some movie. At first it was funny, but as a mom, I try not to laugh in their faces. I do that behind their backs. I grew up in Michigan with tornados, so to see them freaking out over a little rain was rather amusing.

But then the thunder clapped really loudly, and they both jumped into bed with me under the covers. I was tempted to pull a Julie Andrews and start singing "My Favorite Things," but I didn't think this was the time for song. I was actually thrilled because my kids needed me. They were scared, and they came to me first for comfort, bypassing even Grandma and Grandpa. They were crying and wanted to be near me and no one else. They believed I could comfort them in their time of need. It occurred to me that I might actually mean something to them! I held them close, and I was overjoyed.

We cuddled and talked and sang songs and read books. And then eventually the rain stopped. They wanted to sleep with me. I loved it, until they took all my covers and started sprawling out horizontally, kicking me out of any space I occupied.

I got to thinking about when one of them scrapes their finger and needs a bandage. They still ask me to kiss it first, as if I have some kind of healing mom magic. When Lucy was a baby and I traveled a lot, I would come home and she'd be sleeping in her crib. Sometimes I would stand outside her room, waiting for her to make one tiny sound of a whimper or cry. That was my cue to rush in like Wonder Woman. I'd grab her in my arms, rock her back to sleep, kiss her, and sing to her.

I had missed her so much, and I knew she needed me. Even now, when one of my kids cry, it's like something automatic goes off in my brain. I must rescue them and make the hurt go away. I'll do anything to make them feel less pain, even if the owie is invisible to everyone but them. I don't want to see my daughters in any real pain.

I think that's how God feels about us. He's not there to intrude in our lives, uninvited. But as our Father, He is patiently waiting in the wings for us to make one sound…one prayer…one cry for help, and He's there with what we need. Sometimes we cry out to Him because we're in pain and we know there is nothing anyone else can offer us to help. But sometimes we try to handle things ourselves, and we mess up badly.

I know I've had my fair share of problems, and I've gone to friends, family, and even Facebook before I've turned to God. Thank goodness He loves me enough not to ignore me, even when I come to Him last. He has always been there for His children through the ages. Look how many times the Israelites turned their back on God when they were in the desert. I read some of those passages and think, *They are downright rude to the God of all the universe! They are going to be so busted. He should say, "No manna for you tomorrow!"* But God never did that. He always forgave them, always provided for them, and always was a loving Father.

That's the same way I hope to always be with my little caped crusaders. I just hope they stop trying to fly off the highest playground equipment or jumping off my stairs. My medical supplies are getting expensive!

• • •

### TO THINK ON

- When you are hurt, who is the first person you turn to?
- If you need comfort in your life right now, where do you go?
- Can you recall a time your Father God helped heal you when you were hurt?
- Are you able to trust Him to do it again?

• • •

*Dear God,*

*Thank You for creating children as a perfect example of Your love for us. Thanks for always being there for me when I need comfort and healing from all the things that hurt me.*

*In Jesus' name.*

*Amen.*

# HOPE DEFERRED MAKES ME PRAY HARDER

*Hope deferred makes the heart sick,*
*but a longing fulfilled is a tree of life.*

**PROVERBS 13:12**

I've had the privilege of praying with some mighty women in my life. In fact, I've had a group of faithful warriors who have prayed for me throughout my time in ministry. I call them my "Mighty Women." A friend came into my life after my second daughter was born. The nurses rushed Ruby to a place called the neonatal intensive care unit (NICU). After taking my baby home I met a mom named Jen at church whose son was born with challenges. Being a NICU mom is not a club you want to join, and rarely do you get an advance invitation. But after Ruby was out of the hospital, on an oxygen tank and forced to start all kinds of therapy, I immediately needed all the support I could get.

It was comforting to have someone who'd taken up the torch of praying for a sick child. Jen and I got out our swords—our Bibles—and we spoke the Word of God over our children, our families, and every area of our lives. I always felt better after seeing Jen. As they say, iron sharpens iron, and we were really sharp! I joined Jen in the journey, giving her words of encouragement to spur her on to battle for her son's healing, no matter how long it took.

Sometimes you don't need a crowd of people to pray with. If you are fortunate enough to find just one person who will pray with you, consider yourself blessed. I learned a lot from Jen. I learned to use

Scripture to proclaim God's promises. I learned that no matter what it looks like, and no matter what others might say, we can speak the Word of God over any situation and stand in faith. He will work all things together for our good.

That's not just some random cliché. God wrote that down in the Bible for us to comfort and encourage us when needed. Sometimes I would take my Bible over to Jen's house, and we'd march around her living room, praying, proclaiming, and seeking God's face to meet all of our needs. We both chose to fight all the negative predictions about our children's future. We fought with our weapons, our mouths, and our Bibles. I can tell you, looking back on those prayer times, God answered so many of our prayers, big and small. When we needed provision, God provided.

After praying with Jen, I felt like I had just taken my soul to the gym for a spiritual workout. Connecting with her and speaking words of faith made me feel so good. I was so full of faith, I almost expected to come home and see my baby flying through the air or doing algebra!

When we needed peace, God was there. When we needed wisdom and clarity, we found it. We always felt God's sweet presence telling us to keep going. My baby was eventually healed enough to lose the oxygen tank and avoid heart surgery. And the miracles continued. Jen's son enrolled in regular school.

I loved praying with Jen because we always spurred each other on to believe God would move in our lives. I was always on the lookout for those moves. One of the things I've learned is that you usually will find what you are looking for. If you go through life looking to see God do a miracle, even the smallest thing might excite you. If you are looking to see all the tragedies and unanswered prayers, you can see those in wide supply. I know that's why one of the enemy's biggest tactics is to isolate us from other believers who could encourage us. If we are alone, we are more susceptible to hearing the enemy's lies about our situation. We can tune out God's Word and tune into our own feelings. It's a downward spiral from there.

About six years ago, Jen's family moved to Arizona. I tease her, "Sure, that's wonderful, if you don't mind living directly *on* the sun." But

Arizona does remind me of the Bible because every time I'm there in the summer, I know what the fiery furnace feels like. For a while I made a point to visit Jen and her family often, and she also came back to Los Angeles a few times. We prayed together over the phone on a regular basis at first, but life, as it often does, took us in different directions. However I knew she was always one phone call away.

I had the pleasure of taking a girls' trip with her and some friends last summer. Her son was graduating high school, but he still struggled and Jen was seeing a doctor for some heart issues. She said something that stuck in my mind: "I feel like the root of this problem is that my hope deferred made my heart sick."

I didn't quite understand what she meant. She said she'd been struggling all these years, trying to put God on her timeline. She had insisted that God heal her son immediately, but healing had not come. Now she was stressed out emotionally and physically. We prayed for her that night, that she would have peace in the circumstances. I've never seen a mom pray harder for her child than Jen does.

I had a chance to catch up with Jen about a week ago, and she told me how much better she was feeling. Her son was going to take some local college classes, and he was working a part-time job. He still had struggles, but Jen told me she felt rejuvenated, both physically and spiritually. She said she had learned a lot through this latest trial. She was a warrior, but God had taught her this: we can win our real battle against the enemy when we enter into rest.

If we are at rest, then we can trust God has the best plans for our lives. It's okay to be a warrior, and it's okay to hope for a great outcome. But in the end, it's the journey that matters most. We don't want to get to the finish line so worn out and haggard that we aren't any good to anyone. The victory comes in finding rest. And that rest is in our assurance that we serve a loving God who made promises for our lives.

. . .

## TO THINK ON

- Is there any hope deferred in your life that could be making your heart sick? It's okay if there is.

- Do you want to enter into rest? What does real rest look like to you? Maybe curling up in your bed is just what God needs you to do so He can restore you mind, body, and soul?

• • •

*Dear God,*

*You know my heart's desires. Please help me to enter into rest about this situation. I know You have my best interest in mind. Help me wait on You.*

*In Jesus' name.*

*Amen.*

# DEATH, DYING, AND THE SECRET SAUCE

*He will wipe every tear from their eyes. There will
be no more death or mourning or crying or pain, for
the old order of things has passed away.*

**REVELATION 21:4**

One of my dear friends died a few days ago. *Friend* isn't a good enough word; she was like my sister. There is no way to prepare for the moment when someone leaves this earth for good. She was only 33.

It's interesting: after people die, we say all these wonderful things about them and seem to forget any of their weaknesses. But with Amelia, there really is nothing negative to even think about. If angels walked on earth, I can say I met one. I knew Amelia for over a decade as we became friends and then coworkers, and it was my pleasure to have her in my life. She eventually became my personal assistant, and this is not a job for the weak of heart. She basically ran my life for many years, and she knew more about me than…well, me.

Amelia was born with cerebral palsy, and doctors told her mom not to consider regular schooling for her daughter because she would be severely disabled. Well, thank God Sara didn't listen, because her little baby grew up to be homecoming queen and a college graduate. After many employers passed her by because they were afraid of her physical condition, I happily hired her onto our team and we traveled the world together, including New York City, Los Angeles, and Toronto. She used crutches and sometimes a wheelchair, but they didn't slow her down at all. Amelia lived in chronic pain, but she never complained. She made me feel like my problems were of epic importance, even when she was in and out of surgeries. We often joked that if Amelia was going under anesthesia and I texted her for my bank account number, she would still reply.

Four years ago Amelia's health took a severe decline after some unsuccessful surgeries. She was bedridden and in severe pain. There were more surgeries, but the prognosis got worse. Even when she entered hospice care, thousands of others and I never gave up praying for her miracle. She wanted to be healed so badly. I've never seen someone with such a steadfast faith in God's love despite life kicking her down every single day. She wrote blogs about her love for God, and I would visit and lay hands on her and then go home and scream into my pillow at how unfair it was that my friend was suffering with no relief. Even hospice couldn't stop her pain.

I just got the news that another friend of mine named Susan lost her battle with cancer, leaving behind five children and a husband who all prayed for her miracle healing. I talked several times with Susan by phone, reciting Scripture and crying out to God for a breakthrough. She believed God was going to heal her here on earth.

Lucy asked me, "Mommy, how come when we prayed for baby Faith to get healed from cancer, it happened in one month—and when we prayed for Amelia, it never happened?" I was at a loss for words. I'm a Bible-believing, Spirit-filled Christian and I do not know the answer to that question. And spouting something cliché like "God's ways are not our ways" didn't seem appropriate to a ten-year-old who was grieving. I just hugged her and tried not to sob. Amelia was family.

I drove down the road today and started crying because my heart hurt. And then I remembered something amazing that happened last week. Ruby had come to me and said, "I had a dream about Amelia." Ruby is young and didn't understand that Amelia was dying; she just knew we prayed for her every day. Ruby said, "Mommy, I saw Amelia going down a slide and she was happy. Then she walked away and went shopping in this big store." Ruby told me Amelia didn't have her crutches in the dream.

I think Ruby had a vision of Amelia in heaven. I think God gave my daughter a glimpse of Amelia playing in heaven…healed and free and in no pain. Ruby's idea of joy is the slide in our backyard, and Amelia's idea of joy was shopping. Why shouldn't there be malls in heaven where everything is free? That day I texted Amelia about Ruby's dream. Amelia couldn't talk near the end, but she texted me that Ruby's dream gave her chills.

So the truth is, death is real and painful. But the other truth is that heaven is real. Believers like Susan and Amelia are experiencing a joy and a sense of peace we can't even comprehend. I don't know why they had to die so young. I am heartbroken and confused because I did everything in my human power to pray them both back to health. And for someone like me who has seen miracles, it's hard to accept that I lost these two battles.

I don't have the secret sauce when it comes to praying for healing; I just know that God tells us to keep praying. And in their honor, I'm never going to quit. I told Lucy, "Maybe Jesus made Amelia an offer she couldn't refuse." Lucy says there are waterslides in heaven, and I say there are unlimited buffets. Lucy agreed that if all that was true, she wasn't going to be sad because Amelia was with Jesus. And I suspect she is rocking out some serious jumpsuits with no crutches and carrying a gorgeous purse and probably hanging with her new friend Susan. That's the way I like to picture it.

• • •

## TO THINK ON

- What is your idea of heaven?
- How has death affected your life? Has it left you wounded? Angry?
- Can you take those feelings to God and let Him help you process them?

• • •

*Dear God*

*My heart is broken that my loved one is gone. I don't know how to put the pieces back together. But help me not to turn bitter toward You. Help me not to stop believing that You are good and to understand that Your plans are not always my plans.*

*In Jesus' name.*

*Amen.*

# EVERYTHING OLD IS NEW AGAIN

*My command is this: Love each other as I have loved you. Greater love has no one than this: to lay down one's life for one's friends.*

**JOHN 15:12-13**

God has given me wonderful women to link arms with every step of the way. But I've also run the gamut of relationships with friends in my life: good, bad, and not so healthy. Friendship was so much easier when I was a kid. If you didn't get along with another kid, you just got mad and then at recess one of you would ask the other to go on the seesaw together, and all was well in the world once again.

As I sit here writing this, it occurs to me that there are women from my past whom I thought would be with me till the end, and yet for some reason we parted ways. I remember when my very best friend in the whole world and I were both going through some enormous life transitions. Never in my wildest dreams would I have predicted that our friendship would end. We never even had any conflict, but it happened, and it broke my heart. Why would God take away my partner, my shoulder to cry on, my rock? Most of our friendship had been based on being there for each other through severely rough waters (sickness, the death of a loved one, and divorce). I think some of my most intimate friendships through the last decade have been with women who have gone through intense trials, and we were able to bond together and pray and support each other in a special way.

I have another friend I walked with through similar circumstances. She was another rock for me and vice versa. And through a series of events and relocations, we lost touch. I hated it, and I didn't understand why it happened. Was God pulling people out of my life that weren't healthy, or was the enemy pulling away my best friends? Looking back, I can say it might have been a little bit of both. We women can get so intertwined in each other's lives, and we rely so heavily on another person, we forget that God wants that place in our hearts. That's a tough pill to swallow, but it's for our own good. I did learn to lean into God in a deeper and more intimate way. I learned He is the only source of real peace and He wanted to take my sorrows, confusion, and even fears. God longs to become number one.

After some time apart, I picked up the phone and called my BFF one day. I was going through my own painful marriage separation and I really needed my friend. I needed to hear her voice. I needed to hear from her that I was going to be okay because she had been there. And when I called her, she immediately listened, prayed, and did everything she could to help me. With a history like ours, as "battle buddies," I knew we would always be there for one another, even if there had been a big bump in the road. It's not like we immediately picked up where we'd left off, but we did continue to talk. Eventually we went to see each other, and we shared mutual apologies without a lot of unnecessary drama. We had both had some healing in our lives, and today she and I talk often and do life together. Whatever happened in the past is long forgotten.

The other friend I mentioned reached out to me via e-mail not too long ago because she needed some prayer. When you build a deep friendship with somebody, and then that relationship pause button gets pressed, don't assume it's forever. God might have other plans for you both. My friend was at my house tonight for a prayer meeting, and instead of rehashing why we'd drifted apart, I just hugged her and said, "I love you and I'm glad you are here." And I feel like that was a very good start.

We might have a relationship in our lives that, for whatever reason, looks dead. But maybe God just needed us to put it to the side for a season so He could do some healing. Maybe our lives are more like a merry-go-round than a seesaw, and God is orchestrating who gets to ride with us at any given time. Instead of thinking of friendships as completely over, maybe God just had that person in another place for a moment. Maybe she was on her way back to you the whole time, and you just needed to trust God and keep going. He knows who our best playmates should be.

• • •

## TO THINK ON

- Have you had friendships end unexpectedly? How did you handle it?

- Do you think God sometimes weaves us out of relationships for a greater purpose?

- Are there any friendships in your life right now that are pulling you away from a greater dependence on God?

- If so, would you be willing to give that relationship to God to do what's best for both of you?

• • •

*Dear God,*

*Thank You for knowing who I need and when I need them in my life. Please show me if any human relationship takes the place of my communion with You. I ask You to bless all of my friendships, and I give You permission to do what is needed. I want to link arms with the people You know are best for me.*

*In Jesus' name.*

*Amen.*

# THE GREAT BRUNCHCON RACE

*Then Jesus declared, "I am the bread of life.*
*Whoever comes to me will never go hungry, and*
*whoever believes in me will never be thirsty."*

**JOHN 6:35**

am at a phase in my life where things like chocolate pancakes are very exciting to me. The one magical word that gets my juices flowing like no other? *Brunch!* Yes, I like sitting and eating. I think that's why I could never do online dating because my profile would say, "Looking for someone who likes eating brunch and enjoys other sedentary activities such as slow walking and frequenting oyster happy hours."

Well, I found tickets to the mother of all events called BrunchCon. A festival of brunch! I snapped up tickets for myself and my friends Gina and Nicki lickety-split. At church that Sunday I could barely focus on the sermon. I kept picturing waffles and crepes with Nutella and the Willy Wonka experience I was about to have. I couldn't sit still.

I repented to God for leaving the service five minutes early to drive all the way to Long Beach and pick up Gina and Nicki. The event was at a conference center called The Reef, so I left my car at Gina's and we all took an Uber. We arrived a little later than planned, but the event lasted until 4:00 p.m. and that allowed plenty of time to stuff our faces until we hurt. We walked around and saw a grand buffet, but we quickly realized this was not BrunchCon. We walked around, a bit confused, and then asked the hostess where the event was. She said, "You must mean the *other* Reef location in downtown LA."

Downtown LA? You might as well have said Cuba! We were in Long Beach, and it was now 2:40 p.m. Downtown was at least a 45-minute drive *if* you didn't hit traffic. We were stunned. I grabbed a pastry to comfort myself, which Gina pointed out was stealing.

So apparently we had all read the invitation and assumed the location was in Long Beach. As we stood there in defeat, not knowing what to do, I grabbed another jelly roll and raised it in the air like Mel Gibson in *Braveheart*. "Girls," I bellowed, "we paid for these tickets and we are not out yet! My car is super low on gas and we have no time to get gas. Let's call an Uber and make this happen!" So what if we would arrive with only 22 minutes to gorge? We were not quitters! They thought I was a bit off my rocker but agreed to my *I Love Lucy* plan. We got picked up by a nice gentleman from India in the Uber and I'm pretty sure we scared the life out of him. His English wasn't fluent, but Nikki kept giving him hand signals to drive faster and was trying to sound out "pedal to the metal" in sign language. I think he was thrilled to see us get out.

We arrived at 3:33 p.m. and decided we should divide and conquer. The spread was looking rough. The food stations that had probably looked fresh at 9:00 a.m. were now just fragments of leftovers. It wasn't exactly delightful, but we were on a mission. We had to get our money's worth, and nothing was going to stop us! We decided to meet in the middle to share our bounty, and we all advanced toward each other with piles of paper plates and sample cups.

The first to start the avalanche was Gina as she and her "tower of brunch" started to tumble when we got to the table. I was laughing so hard that I lost grip on my soggy avocado toast and macaroons and my plates tumbled too. Nicki, who had been concentrating on making friends with the bartender, tried to come to our rescue. I called out that the 30-second rule was in play, and did my best to scrape the quiches and waffles from the table. We ate as much as we could and stuffed the rest into our swag bags like bootleggers. We ate and laughed till we were ill.

Then we had the pleasure of going *all* the way back to Long Beach to get my car, and then I had to drive *all* the way home feeling disoriented, stuffed, and slipping into a food coma.

Was it worth it?

Well, the Uber rides cost more than our tickets, but yes!

I wonder what God was thinking about my obsession that day to make sure I got my brunch on. Sure, I showed up for church. But was my passion for the spiritual food I was receiving even in the same stratosphere as my excitement for flavored sparkling organic waters?

It reminded me that even things that seem innocent can distract us in ways that take us away from the nourishment God has for us. When Jesus met the woman at the well in John 4, He said to her, "Everyone who drinks of this water will be thirsty again, but whoever drinks of the water that I will give him will never be thirsty again. The water that I will give will become in him a spring of water welling up to eternal life" (verses 13-14 ESV).

I know God was probably shaking His head in amusement at my bad sitcom of a day. But in the end it was a good lesson that I don't want to be so off-balance that anything, even avocado toast, gets in the way of me getting my real nourishment from Him.

•  •  •

## TO THINK ON

- Do you remember a time you were so focused on something that it seemed ridiculous? How did it work out for you?

- Can you think of anything in your life right now that is off-balance? Maybe it's not about food, but sports or another activity is taking up a little too much space in your head and time in your schedule?

- Ask God for perspective and wisdom, and He will give it to you.

• • •

*Dear God,*

*Thank You that You care enough about me to show me where I am off-balance. Please shine a light on any activities or interests, however small, that are taking me away from communing in an intentional way with You. Give me the strength to make any changes You know will be best. I'm sorry I don't always put You first. Thanks for giving me a new day to try again.*

*In Jesus' name.*

*Amen.*

*P.S. Thank You for inventing avocado toast.*

# MONSTERS IN MY BED

*Whoever dwells in the shelter of the Most High
will rest in the shadow of the Almighty.*

**PSALM 91:1**

Yes, what my mother told me was true: there *are* monsters in my bedroom, and they are scary.

There is a big one and a little one, and they creep into my room after I have gone to sleep. They take over my bed and torment me through the night. They kick me and lie on me, and the big one elbowed me in the nose last night. It's not charming at all when the minions sneak into my bed because they want to "cuddle," as they claim. They just say that to gain entrance to sharing my fluffy bed and my TV!

Sometimes my youngest, Ruby, will say, "Mom, let's have a cuddle party and watch *The Golden Girls*," and it starts out adorable. But if I let her remain there, I'm in for a night of snoring and restless body syndrome. It's a war zone! But people have warned me that there could come a time when I will lie awake one night missing the sound of the patter of little feet climbing into my bed and fighting ferociously about who gets to be next to Mom.

We moms spend our days being taxi driver, short-order cook, tutor, and maid without much thanks. But at the end of the night, when I see that these little monsters' biggest desire is to cuddle up next to or on top of their mommy, I just don't have the desire to shoo them away; in fact, I hug one or both of them when they are sleeping and stare at how beautiful and peaceful they are. I *love* when they are sleeping! And I put my arms around them and squeeze them tightly. I pray over them and their futures and know there is literally nowhere else in the universe I would rather be.

How long will this last? I'm not sure. I told Lucy we were going to be dorm-mates in college, and she thinks I'm kidding. I bask in these moments, between getting beaten up by arms and elbows, where I feel so utterly loved and at peace. I know that despite anything else I've done in this world, these are my most prized possessions. (Yes, possessions! I made them, and I have the scars to prove it!) When they have nightmares, they need me. When they are lonely, they want to be near me. But these moments are not taking place during the busyness of their days. They aren't stopping to tell me they are grateful for the fact that they have clothes on their backs and dinner on the table. They are too busy jumping rope, watching the Muppets on YouTube, and living very content lives.

I like to spend time reading my Bible and praying in my bed. It's my coziest spot. And at night before my kids go to sleep they come into my room and we do our devotions together. My bed has become a communal place of comfort and joy and lots of Hallmark Channel. It's my happy place. So of course the kids would rather be in Mommy's bed than their own. I wonder if all the prayer time and Bible reading has made that space feel extra special? God does promise us that if we draw near to Him, He will draw near to us. And isn't that what we all need?

I bet God feels the same way about me as I do my little monsters. He's always excited when I want to spend time with Him and read His Word and have moments of stillness so He can love on me. But most of my time is spent juggling carpool, work, friendships, obligations, and appointments, being busy and a bit ungrateful, like my kids can be. I should be thankful for the simple things like getting up every day healthy, with a beautiful bed to sleep in and good food on my table (thank you, Costco). I've taught my kids to declare something about the goodness of God every morning. If I can learn with my children to start and end my day with gratefulness, I know I'm winning at least half the battle.

So today I declare to the Lord that I am grateful for my 800-thread-count Egyptian cotton sheets from Costco! Amen! Thank You, Jesus!

• • •

## TO THINK ON

- Do you have a happy place where you can pray and spend time with God? (If it's your bathtub with your Bible and Nutella, I'm not judging!)

- Have you considered starting your day with declaring the goodness of God? Do you think it would change how you go about your day?

• • •

*Dear Lord,*

*Today I will see the goodness, the favor, and the glory of You. I will be grateful for all You've blessed me with and look for specific opportunities to see You at work in my life. Thank You for all that You've done for me and that Your mercies are new every morning.*

*In Jesus' name.*

*Amen.*

Day 15

# HERE I GO ROUND THE MERRY-GO-ROUND

## And Round and Round...

*When you pass through the waters, I will be with you;*
*and when you pass through the rivers,*
*they will not sweep over you.*

**ISAIAH 43:2**

Remember the playgrounds of your childhood? When I was six, I could play on the merry-go-round for hours, and I would be happily content going nowhere. But now I'm overprogrammed, overstressed, and overscheduled, and completely exhausted, 24/7.

I hope it's okay to be that honest, even though you bought my book thinking I had some answers. I actually do know some answers; I'm just having some difficulty putting them into action. I think I'm fatigued from reading and planning better ways to have a balanced life of rest and security. I know I should eat more kale. I should go to bed without my cell phone. I should put aside a certain time of day for quiet time with the Lord. There are women who do *all* these things. They are also on Pinterest and make farm-to-table meals seven days a week. I love these women. I buy their books and read their recipes for success. But I am not one of them, no matter how hard I try.

I hate green veggies, and I hate getting up at dawn. I have an uncontrollable habit of scrolling through my phone at all hours of the night.

It's not like I love it. It's just a bad habit and I haven't replaced it with anything healthy. I'm the one putting myself on the merry-go-round, and I'm the one choosing *not* to get off. Will I ever learn? Could today be the day?

I have moments of greatness. I just went to a conference for about a week, and I spent morning, noon, and night listening to incredible Christian speakers. I had hit such a wall that I hopped a plane to Dallas because that's where Jesus lives (the higher the hair, the closer to God). It was a good decision. I needed to get out of my routine and devote some time to the simple message of Jesus. I was reminded of the message God wants us to know, and it's a message that has *never* changed. He loves me unconditionally, and there is nothing I can do to make Him love me more (even if I served in youth ministry) or make Him love me less (even if I became addicted to Facebook). He's not mad at me when I spin around like a kid on a merry-go-round or a hamster on a wheel. He just feels sad for me because He knows a better plan for my day.

When my kids do something that's going to end up causing big trouble for them but they *refuse* to listen to me, I want to say to them, "Look, I'm a little further along in this show you call life. I'm on season 40, and you're just on season 10. There are a lot of plot twists I could help you with, if you would *let me*!" Don't you think if God decided to come down from heaven and talk to us in our homes, He would have some better time management skills for us? Such as, "Start your day with Me! I promise there is so much I want to share with you. I have so much I could teach you and help you with. Your problems are not a surprise to Me, My darling. Stop trying to be a Marvel superhero, and stop thinking that you can solve everything by yourself. Stop asking the opinions of friends, colleagues, and people you have never met except on a screen."

Sometimes I go to bed praying but wake up feeling guilty because I fell asleep with my Bible on my face. But I heard a pastor say once, "Do you think you'd be mad if one of your babies fell asleep cuddling up in your arms?" When we read His Word and pray to Him, we can feel like we're cuddling up in His arms. Maybe He knew I needed the sleep.

But here's the thing that the enemy doesn't want any of us to know: since God is not human, we do not run out of chances with Him. We can always keep trying and stretching ourselves to draw closer to Him, and He will be right there. Sometimes He'll have us reach a little further and a little higher, but it's for our growth.

When I was teaching my girls to swim across the pool to me, as they got to be stronger swimmers, I would move a few inches farther away. Before they knew it, they could swim the entire length of the pool before grabbing for my hands. It was slow and intentional growth. I saw them getting stronger each time they tried. I knew they could do it. I knew no matter what, I was *never* going to let them drown. If they sank too far in the water, I would be there to catch them—and that's exactly how God is with us. I just hope He doesn't have a highlights reel submitted to Him by my guardian angels when I get to heaven. Because if He does, as they say in *I Love Lucy*, "I'll have a lot of 'splaining to do!"

• • •

## TO THINK ON

- How busy are you really?
- Stop right now and take an inventory of your life.
- If it feels exhausting and overwhelming, ask God to help.

• • •

*Dear God,*

*I know I've prayed this a thousand times, but I need You to help me slow down and find some balance. I need You to help me consult You before I consult the people and things of this world for answers. Please speak loudly so I can hear You clearly today. I love You.*

*In Jesus' name.*

*Amen.*

# FEAR AND BASEBALL

*Even though I walk*
*through the darkest valley,*
*I will fear no evil,*
*for you are with me;*
*your rod and your staff,*
*they comfort me.*

**PSALM 23:4**

If you asked me the question, "What are you so afraid of?" and I gave you an honest answer, it might come down to one word: *everything*. I can call myself a strong, fearless woman and preach the gospel across the globe, but one strike from the enemy in my personal life and I could be on the ground looking for Snickers under my bed and doing the ugly cry. When I was a kid, I played softball, and every time I got up to bat, I was plagued with the fear I would strike out and let my team down. The struggle was real. And I wanted to win so we could get free pizza!

I believe fear is one of the most powerful weapons Satan uses against us. Fear of the unknown, fear of change, fear of failure. I've struggled with all of these in this rat race we call the human existence. I'll be going about my day swimmingly: devotional done, Bible read, prayers said, kids washed and cleaned—and one email can send my life into a tailspin.

Yesterday I learned that the beloved principal of my daughter's tiny little school is leaving after 30 years. Three teachers are leaving as well—and school starts in three weeks. My youngest has had a few learning challenges, and this principal was her champion and advocate and even pulled her out of class to personally tutor her during the day. I tried my best not to go into freak-out mode and to calm myself as I read texts from other parents doing the same thing. I tried to breathe and repeat what I know to be true: "God, You are good. God, You are in charge of my daughters' lives. I put my trust in You." Eventually I felt a bit calmer.

But then more texts and emails came. I decided to partner my prayer with sushi, and that helped too. After all, Jesus served fish. When I went to bed, the spirit of fear kept trying to rear its ugly head. I played out the best- and worst-case scenarios in my head. (I have this gift/curse of having a mind that can go warp speed ahead in 30 seconds. Sound familiar?) This is not my first rodeo with school disruptions, but I am trying desperately to deal with this newest hurdle in a healthier way.

Then this morning my mother called to let me know her brother had been admitted to the hospital with intestinal blockage and my father was at the doctor with a long-term health concern and they were considering admitting him as well. I only knew to do three things:

1. Breathe.

2. Recite and remember what I know to be true: "God gave us a spirit not of fear but of power and love and self-control" (2 Timothy 1:7 esv).

3. Repeat.

When I meditated on this verse, God showed me some other truths as well. I do not put my faith in one teacher or principal or even one doctor. I put my faith in God. Before my kids were born, He had the perfect school picked out for them. Before the earth was formed, God knew the perfect doctors and even hospitals that would help my family. My job in this equation is not to do the thing the enemy wants me do, which is give in to fear and get comfortable with the feelings of anxiety and worry and paralysis. Then the enemy wins.

No matter what curveballs my daily life is throwing at me, I can be a steady player when I am assured that God knows how the game is going to play out. He just asks me to keep praying and playing and stepping up to bat. My baseball-playing friend told me that the secret to hitting a curveball is timing. You have to wait just a little bit longer before you swing. I think that's the way it is with fear. If you swing at your emotions too early, as soon as that curveball comes at you, you're going to miss or possibly get hurt.

But if you realize there is a precise plan to waiting (praying, remembering God's promises), you have a much better chance of hitting a home run.

• • •

## TO THINK ON

- How is fear stopping you today from living a full life? Take the issue you are fearful about and break it down.

- Who is giving you this fear? Is it your mind? The enemy? Both?

- What promise can you find in God's Word to combat this fear? Say that verse out loud, over and over.

• • •

*Dear Lord,*

*You have not given me a spirit of fear but of power, love, and a sound mind. I rebuke these lies the enemy is speaking to me about my situation and I put my full trust in You for the best outcome. Please continue to guide me and give me peace today and every day.*

*In Jesus' name.*

*Amen.*

Day 17

# THE POWER OF NO

*I will instruct you and teach you in the way you should go;*
*I will counsel you with my loving eye on you.*

**PSALM 32:8**

There are words in the English language that excite me, such as *brunch* and *free admission*. But one of the most powerful words in my life and career is this one: *no*. As an actress in Hollywood, I'm used to hearing that word after auditions and meetings. But what do I say when I'm offered something from the cool kids' table in show business? Do I grab it and run and deal with the consequences later? Do I have the strength to say no?

In my early days as an actress, it wasn't hard to turn down roles that were inappropriate, even though my agent said I was making a mistake. (The film was with Charlie Sheen! True story! #winning) Later on, a producer saw my comedy and decided the "character" I was playing was perfect for a sitcom. I had to break the news to him: all my jokes were real! I had meetings on the top floors of fancy office buildings, and they set up showcases for producers. They gave feedback that they liked me, but the producer was a little concerned I was "too Christian." They wanted my funny Christian sitcom character to start the first episode by seeking my pastor's advice on whether I should get a boob job. I had to politely say no thanks.

Then things got more complicated. I was courted by the biggest Christian women's tour in existence, and they invited me to join up with them for possibly 32 cities. But the executives decided they wanted to be more seeker-friendly, and they asked if I could tone down some of the Christianity in my act. No, I'm not kidding, people. That one hurt. This was a well-established, top-tier organization that had bowed to the idea that less faith might mean more money! Did we ever think we'd see the day that Christians were asking me to be...*less Christian*?

I felt so wounded for my Savior that people of faith were ashamed of Him. They wanted to be "undercover" Christians so they wouldn't be offensive. Didn't Jesus tell us that the gospel *is* offensive? Once again, I had to use that little word *no*. Yes, people thought I was crazy.

I had to get quiet with the Lord each time I faced a decision and tune out what the world was telling me to do. People were saying, "This is the big break you've been waiting for. Say yes and don't worry about a little compromise." I have a million of these stories.

This happened again last week. I got offered a lead role in a sitcom. I was about to say yes, and the executives were ready to fly me out to the East Coast to shoot the pilot. Then I got the full script and read it over, and it was 100 percent clean—nothing compromising at all. But I can't tell you it was good. It was painful. I wanted to like it, but artistically, I would have been selling my soul for a paycheck. Just because something is clean does not make it good. God wants quality in everything we do.

I had to pray about it and see how I felt in my heart about putting my name on this project. I didn't have peace. I prayed all night, and I knew if I said yes, my stomach would be in knots.

I called the producer to tell her I didn't think I could do it, and guess what? She literally tripled my salary! Yes, *triple*! Not that it was that big to begin with, but you get the point. The enemy was dangling a carrot in front me and expecting me to bite. I'm a single mom, summer is a slow season, and I needed that money. But at what cost?

The Bible teaches, "What good will it be for someone to gain the whole world, yet forfeit their soul? Or what can anyone give in exchange for their soul? For the Son of Man is going to come in his Father's glory with his angels, and then he will reward each person according to what they have done" (Matthew 16:26-27). I don't want to have to explain to Jesus all the bad choices of my career or my life. I've done enough other stupid stuff that I'll be talking about. There isn't enough money or fame or gratification that can make compromise worth it, especially when God is telling us to be strong and hold our ground.

When considering if a little compromise is okay, imagine if I served you the most delicious bowl of your favorite homemade ice cream and I included just a little dog food in it. Would you eat it?

As I write this I can honestly tell you for every no, there was a bigger, better God-made yes waiting on the other side. I just have to trust Him and take one step at a time.

I never did have a taste for dog food!

* * *

## TO THINK ON

- Can you remember a time in your life where the world wanted you to say yes and God wanted you to say no? What happened?

- What about now? Are there any situations in your life that you know in your heart are compromises you shouldn't make? Are you willing to trust God? Maybe you are having to make a decision about something big like a job offer, or maybe it is something smaller like a certain TV show or film you feel you shouldn't watch. God can take care of it if you let Him.

* * *

*Dear Lord,*

*Please shine a light on my life and the areas where there might be a "little dog food" thrown in. I don't want anything in my life that is unpleasing to You or not good for me. Help me to be strong the next time I have a tough decision. Help me tune out the world and hear You clearly. You will guide me in the way I should go. And it will be good. Thanks, God.*

*In Jesus' name.*

*Amen.*

# THE SKY IS FALLING AND SO IS MY HAIR

*So humble yourselves under the mighty power of God,*
*and at the right time he will lift you up in honor. Give all*
*your worries and cares to God, for he cares about you.*

**1 PETER 5:6-7 NLT**

Sometimes I have first-world problems and I'm completely convicted about it. Today was Jerusalem hot in LA and I was in TJ Maxx trying to cool off, feeling sticky and miserable. I passed some Frisbees, and I was reminded of these sweet kids I met in Africa once on a mission trip who ate their meals off of Frisbees because they didn't have enough plates. I get it: some of my complaints aren't that big.

But just because the world doesn't classify all my woes as "red alert," does that mean they are any less a big deal to me?

Lately I've been quizzing all of my girlfriends on the big question: "How much hair do you lose in the shower?" For whatever reason I'm going through one of those shedding seasons with my hair, and even though I've been through it before, it always scares me. I wake up and look in the mirror with terror, worrying that my hair is getting thinner. My bathroom floor seems to be covered with stray hairs, and I'm obsessed with measuring the size of the hair ball I lose after a washing. I've even studied my eyebrows to make sure they aren't thinning out too.

The funny thing is, after some careful surveys, I have deduced I am not alone, and most of my friends are worried on some level about this very same issue, and none of us actually look like we're suffering from alopecia or female pattern hair loss. But the camaraderie doesn't take away the worry. I can't seem to get over the fact that my hair is falling out more than normal and there is no medical cause. My thyroid is normal, so I can't even blame my hair loss or weight gain on that! I still want a shirt that says, "I'm Not Fat, It's My Thyroid!" though.

This hair loss plagues me every day, and I'm taking so many vitamins I could lift a car. I don't know what else to do except wait for everything to go back to normal. I know it will. I've been through this routine before, but it still feels just as worrisome as the first time it happened.

Maybe you have something in your life that is troubling you in a similar way. Maybe it's a physical malady that doesn't seem to be going away. Maybe it's a financial worry or something that's keeping you up at night that no one knows about. God cares about the cries of your heart even if they are unspoken. He cares about you, your pets, your loved ones, and all that concerns you. He cares about the hairs on your head and knows exactly how many there are at any given time. He even wrote about it in His Word: "Indeed, the very hairs of your head are all numbered. Don't be afraid; you are worth more than many sparrows" (Luke 12:7).

I should write that verse out and tape it to my bathroom mirror. And also I think I'll add Isaiah 43:19: "See, I am doing a new thing! Now it springs up; do you not perceive it?"

No, I may not perceive it, but I can assure you God is doing a new thing in me—all of me—even the little baby hairs on my head. There is new growth. I can be sure of that. Now, can we do something about them being gray? God is the God of miracles, after all! He did invent Ms. Clairol.

. . .

## TO THINK ON

- What is there in your life that is keeping you up at night with worry? Is it something you need wisdom about?

- Can you ask God to show you how much He cares about everything that concerns you? And can you ask God to help you find peace in the waiting?

• • •

*Dear God,*

*Thank You that even though You are the God of all creation, You care so much about me that You know the number of hairs on my head. Please help me not worry so much and help me realize that You have everything under control. When You are doing a new thing in me, please show me how to perceive it.*

*In Jesus' name.*

*Amen.*

# IT'S NOT YOU, IT'S ME!

## OR IS IT?

*Be tolerant with one another and forgive one another whenever
any of you has a complaint against someone else. You must
forgive one another just as the Lord has forgiven you.*

**COLOSSIANS 3:13 GNT**

t's 4:15 a.m. and I want to pull out my hair. But as you read in a previous chapter, that is not something I can afford to do right now. I wish I wasn't so overly sensitive. Or maybe I actually have a righteous reason to be upset. But even if I do, I hate it! Why do people have to say mean things and why do I care so much? In the situation I am going through right now, the hurtful words are coming from someone I care about deeply and have had a wonderful personal and professional relationship with for a long time.

Maybe that is why it hurts so much. I don't know whether to scream or cry or go to my fridge and binge-eat ice cream. I want peace in my life in every area. If one relationship is off, it literally keeps me up at night. And believe me, tonight I'm fully aware it is *not* God that is keeping me up. It's either me being in my flesh or the enemy talking smack to me about how awful the email exchanges with my friend were, so much so that I had to shut off my phone and my computer so I could breathe and walk away. But I woke up at 3:00 a.m. wide awake and could not avoid checking to see if this person had a response to my last email telling them my side of things. Why can't we go back to being cavemen and hit each other over the head with a bat and be done with it? That's how they did it in the cartoons, and it seemed to work out just fine.

We women also tend to have that lovely way of taking everything personally. When I'm wounded, I want to run away from the whole situation. Some words were said about me that cut me emotionally, and on top of that (in my humble opinion) were not even close to true.

I am wrestling with how I should respond. As a Christian, what does God want me to do? And more importantly, how do I get over these very raw and real emotions of anger and betrayal? I have a right to feel any way I want, but what I do with those feelings is the key.

Can I be like David and scream out at the top of my lungs in frustration? I guess I could, but I'd wake my kids. However, right now that might be my best option. God can take it. He knows my heart is sad. I just want to say to Him, "God, why are people so mean to me at times when I don't deserve it? Why does it have to hurt so much? Couldn't You have made me with thicker skin? And why are relationships so complicated?"

I wish I could be more like Jesus. I mean, Jesus knew Judas was going to betray Him to the point of death and He just let him chill with the disciples the whole time He was in ministry without ever saying *one* word about it until the Last Supper. And even then Jesus had so much class, He didn't call Judas aside and tell him off or call out Judas by name.

I want to be kind and forgiving, but I feel like a big loser right now. I feel like that little girl who got bullied on the playground. That whole saying about sticks and stones is absolutely a lie. Words will always hurt me when the words are hurtful. So what am I going to do? God gives us options. We can pick and choose who we are close with and we can pick the battles that are worth fighting. We don't have to be friends with everyone. But when conflict arises with true friendships, I believe it's worth working through and not letting the enemy win.

I am going to choose to take all my feelings to God because they are only hurting me more getting bottled up inside my brain. I need to think, *What would Jesus do?* in the literal sense and come as close as possible to imitating His example.

Walking in love isn't always easy, but in our Savior's strength, we can do it. And trust me, if I can do this, you can too!

• • •

## TO THINK ON

- When someone says or does something that hurts you, what is your first reaction?

- Do you find yourself acting impulsively or taking time to think things through before speaking?

- Have you encountered a hurtful situation in your life where you had to ask yourself, "What would Jesus do?" Did you try to emulate Him in your actions?

• • •

*Dear Lord,*

*You know my aching heart. You don't want to see me suffering. Please take this hurt that I am feeling and do with it what is best. I don't want to carry it anymore. Please heal the places in my heart that are feeling broken and show me how to walk in love. Christ died for me and gave me the cross to lay my burdens on it. Help me do that right so I can receive Your peace. And thanks for loving me when I've been completely unlovable.*

*In Jesus' name.*

*Amen.*

## TOP TEN THINGS I WANT
## MY DAUGHTERS TO KNOW

1. Matching clothes are overrated. If you got dressed by yourself, I count that as a victory and I think you have an amazing sense of eclectic style.

2. Brushing your teeth and flossing really do matter because someday you are going to have to pay your own dental bills.

3. There is no such thing as the laundry fairy who magically picks up your clothes from the hamper and transports them back to your room, clean and folded. That's me! That's *all* me! You're welcome.

4. I love that you believe in Santa Claus. I hope you never stop believing, even if I have to sneak Christmas presents into your dorm room. P.S. The Easter bunny is not real. He was just trying to steal the spotlight from Jesus' big weekend.

5. When you come into my bedroom at 3:00 a.m. and I look mad, I secretly love it because that's one of the only times you are still enough for me to cuddle you.

6. When you ask me deep life questions, most of the time I'm just winging it. Please fact-check Mommy's answers with Google or your dad. But babies do come from a stork. That I know.

7. I may not make you fancy scrapbooks, but someday you can check my Facebook and see that I tagged you in all your milestones. You were adorable! And thank goodness your nana made you scrapbooks. #motherhoodblessed

8. Other mommies probably don't get their lasagna out of an orange Stouffers box, but it was good enough for my mom, and it's good enough for me.

9. I fear that you will become smarter than me any day

now, so that is why I never let you win at checkers or
cards. I can't do your math homework even now. But I do
appreciate it every time you help me program the DVR
and use the Roku.

10. You are my favorite companions. There is no place on this
planet I would rather be on a Saturday night than curled
up on the couch with you guys, watching a *Golden Girls*
marathon or a Hallmark movie, and eating popcorn. I
plan to do this forever with you. Even when you are in
college. I wasn't kidding about that roommate thing!

# MILLENNIAL CHURCH

*There is neither Jew nor Gentile, neither slave nor free, nor is there male and female, for you are all one in Christ Jesus.*

**GALATIANS 3:28**

People make fun of Los Angeles. They call it Sodom and Gomorrah. But surprisingly, we have a *ton* of churches. They just happen to have names like Bread, Evergreen, Reality, Forks and Knives... three out of the four I just listed are *real*. And in the seasons where I've had to look for a church, it's been interesting. I came to a couple of conclusions. One of them is LA is filled with wonderful places of worship, but a good amount of them require me to own a lot more pairs of leather pants and many wardrobe items I threw out in the '90s.

I'm in a weird season of my life right now. I am a single mom, I am over 30, and I am under 60. I sometimes feel like the odd man out in church circles. I'm too old for singles ministry and too not-married for everything else.

I used to be in an amazing house church led by two of my favorite people in the world, who shall remain nameless because they hate it when I brag about them. When our home church decided not to meet any longer, we all went into mourning. It literally took me years to plug into a church where there were pews and instruments and I had to show up on time. House church was sort of a "Sunday Funday," all hours' occasion with lots of food and not too many rules, except you had to come with an open heart willing to hear from Jesus. It was a pivotal time in my development as a Christian and as someone in ministry. I'm forever grateful.

It was tough trying to find a new church. I felt like I was on *House Hunters*.

I remember visiting this one church that meets in an LA nightclub. My friend invited me, and I knew I had the wardrobe for at least one Sunday (all black, of course—even the kids). When I walked in, I was immediately wondering if I'd happened to walk into a heavy metal rock concert by mistake. But I heard the name Jesus shouted loudly, so I continued to look for a seat. I also was struck by the fact that my presence had clearly brought the age demographic up by at least ten years. Did they need elders? I started looking for earplugs.

I was trying not to be distracted by the real-life Barbie on the stage singing with her back-up dancers…I mean, worship team. She was so stunning and so full of Jesus it was hard to hate her for being a size 0. These two young dudes were next to me, and the one right beside me had been obviously dragged there or perhaps bribed. He was on his phone 90 percent of the time.

The sermon was amazing, once I got past the fact that everyone looked like they just walked out of a photo shoot for Abercrombie & Fitch. What I saw when I looked around were millennials crying out to God, taking their faith seriously and worshiping with wild abandon. (Was I doing that in my twenties? Don't ask.) It was very moving to watch.

And at the end the worship leader asked us to hold hands and she started to talk about salvation. I gave this punk rocker next to me a maternal look and he grabbed my hand. She said, "If you want Jesus to be the ruler of your life, squeeze someone's hand right now!" I almost fainted when this kid next to me squeezed my hand. Was this really happening? I was freaking out with joy. I started to tear up. I wanted to hug him so badly, but he would have run screaming and probably changed his mind. I was actually experiencing this guy giving his life to Jesus and it was incredible. People came over and prayed with him, and I gave his friend a high five with my eyes. I'm chill that way. I felt overwhelmed with emotion and convicted at the same time. Who was I to judge this type of "cool kids" church experience when God knew what this group needed. Maybe it wasn't for me, but I'm sure glad I showed up that day. I witnessed a miracle in leather pants.

I eventually found a church home. It wasn't exactly what I would have predicted, considering that this church has about 1,500 members and 1,497 of them are black American. But hey, God knew I needed something fun. When my friend invited me to Center of Hope, I showed up and got a bunch of hugs from older black American ladies who looked at me as though I were lost, but they were happy to see me. I heard this crazy, hilarious, incredible Pastor Dixon preach and I was hooked. After the service he came out with a bag of potato chips and met me and as they say, the rest is church history. He even asked me to share my daughter's testimony. I walked on stage the next Sunday and said, "Well, I guess I won the raffle for new members!" They were the best crowd ever!

My church has Grammy-winning artists doing worship, and when we like something, our pastor says we should stand up and shout and clap. It's a great workout. We have a DJ after service, and we drink lemonade and do the hustle together. I love my church and can't wait to get there on Sundays. I think God meant for us to have a ball in His house. My best friend there is named Barbara and she's 75. I'm in with the cool girls, and they like whatever I wear; I'm young and trendy to them. I'm always in the live streams. They need me for diversity! And I know I am home.

$$\bullet \quad \bullet \quad \bullet$$

## TO THINK ON

- What is your church life like? Are you happy? Do you look forward to going to church? If not, why?

- Would you be open if God were to ask you to change churches? Could you be open-minded about where He wanted to take you?

• • •

*Dear God,*

*Help me remember that Your children come in all colors, shapes, and sizes. There will not be denominations in heaven. Help me to be in a church where I can thrive and learn more about You. If I'm not in a church where I can grow, will You please give me the strength to consider other options? It can be scary, but I know You have a place where You want me to be.*

*In Jesus' name.*

*Amen.*

Day 21

# IT'S NOT GOSSIP IF
# YOUR HEAD IS BOWED

*Those who consider themselves religious and yet
do not keep a tight rein on their tongues deceive
themselves, and their religion is worthless.*

**JAMES 1:26**

love catching my mother in sin. One time I heard her on the phone
with a friend talking about another friend's "issues" and I busted
her. I said, "Mom, you can't talk about someone else's issues. You
are a Christian!" She said, "Baby, we don't have issues. We have prayer
requests. I just needed to know how to pray."

When I started taking my faith seriously, the number one thing
God convicted me of was my mouth. I have always been an excellent
and highly entertaining storyteller. But just because it's funny doesn't
mean I should share it. Or just because it's dramatic doesn't mean I
need to reenact it. But I brought so much joy to people with my stories!
It was so very hard for me to catch myself in this sinful habit. I didn't
really want to stop when I didn't feel like I was hurting anybody. And
my best audience was my closest friends. I had a bad habit of calling
them when I felt wronged or slighted all in the name of "I need advice"
but that wasn't true. I just wanted them to tell me I'm right.

I wasn't being malicious, but I'd recount the situation under the
disguise of asking for their advice. Maybe I really did want advice—or
maybe I just wanted to tell my side of a story so they could reaffirm that

1. The situation was not my fault.

2. The other person was crazy and owed me an apology.

3. I was a saint for not retaliating after being soooooooooooooo wronged.

I think my gossip habit stemmed from a deep-seated need to be told I'm right. So now that I'm supposedly a mature Christian, how do I deal with drama? Do I run and tell Jesus all about it? I try to, but I usually end up muttering to Him something like, "You saw that, right? Are You going to deal with them since You won't let me?" I still struggle with situations that give me knots in my stomach, and I *truly* want advice on how to handle my frustration. What can be done without hurting someone?

So I came up with this plan. When tempted to gossip, I call a friend and say, "I have a situation with my friend Kimi and I'm only going to tell you facts. Then I want you to tell me the most godly and appropriate way to deal with my feelings." The genius idea? Her name isn't Kimi, it's actually...Ha-ha, gotcha! By not revealing the name of the person I'm having a conflict with, I am able to discuss calmly what happened without feeling guilty. And in the end my friend tells me it's all my stuff that's upsetting me and really not the other person much at all.

In today's social media, internet-trolling, mean-spirited world, gossip is a blood sport, and I don't want to be an all-star player. So how do we resist when "everybody's" doing it?

Just know when someone says something mean-spirited about another person and then ends it with, "We need to pray for them," it's still mean-spirited. Praying doesn't make it okay to gossip. Do you think the Proverbs 31 Woman was tempted to chew the fat around the watering well with the other ladies and talk about whose husband was being more useless at the city gate?

So the test I give myself when I'm tempted to discuss another person is to ask myself, "Could Jesus be in on this conversation and say it was okay?" We don't have to keep all our feelings inside when we're hurt and struggling, but we do need to be strategic about who we share them with and how. Like, one time my friend…Come on, did you really just fall for that? If you want to hear all the good stuff, come to one of my next shows. I tell juicy stories for a living!

• • •

## TO THINK ON

- How much is gossip a part of your life? Do you have friends who constantly drag you into gossip?

- If so, how do you handle it? Do you go with the flow to get the juicy info?

- Have you considered this person might gossip about you if they gossip about others?

- Do you check yourself before you overshare?

• • •

*Dear God,*

*It's hard to find the line between asking for advice or expressing concern and actually gossiping about another person. Please show me when I'm about to cross that line in my conversations and give me the tools I need to keep my mouth shut. If I have something juicy to vent about, remind me that You are there to listen and then nobody gets hurt. And besides, You are the one who can change my hurting or angry heart.*

*In Jesus' name.*

*Amen.*

# I DIDN'T MAKE CHEERLEADING AND I'M STILL NOT OVER IT!

*Therefore, there is now no condemnation
for those who are in Christ Jesus.*

**ROMANS 8:1**

When people ask me why I chose a career in stand-up comedy, I reply, "Isn't it obvious? I didn't make cheerleading!" After all, you don't become a stand-up comic because you were prom queen. If comics had perfect childhoods, what would we talk about on stage? Good comedy comes from pain!

You'd think after having a successful career in film and television and raising two great kids I'd be over my rejection issues. I thought I was. Until recently. I got a letter from a pastor in the mail. He said, "It was such a joy to have you at our event. I thought I'd send along some of the comment cards for your viewing." Immediately I was paralyzed with fear. This had happened before. I would read 27 comments about how wonderful and funny I was and even inspiring, and one old lady would say, "She was too loud" and my entire day would be ruined.

Why do we always seem to focus on the negative about ourselves instead of the positive? I truly believe it's one of the enemy's greatest tactics to make us feel less than and rejected. If we feel we're not worthy of love here on earth, we certainly can't be worthy of a heavenly Father who is grace and mercy. If we feel rejected, we're more likely to make bad choices to be accepted by others or isolate ourselves from other people so we won't get hurt. That rejection feeling is a powerful thing and can be a hindrance toward living the full life of love God intended for us.

And as we all know, the enemy can plant those lies of rejection in a very vicious way, even from a young age. Maybe we had adults speak things over us as kids that were demeaning, or maybe we were bullied by other kids. Maybe we listened to the voice in our heads telling us no matter what we did, we'd never be pretty enough for anyone to love us. If we look at the Bible and what God continually says about us, we can realize these lies of rejection are an act of war from Satan. He wants to steal, kill, and destroy our lives, and that includes the way we feel about ourselves. His ultimate goal is that we reject the Father who loved us first. But we won't let that happen.

We can read accounts of people in the Bible who did horrible acts, and I can bet a lot of them were based in rejection. Saul was terribly insecure and worried that David was going to overthrow his throne, so he tried to kill his faithful servant more than once. In the book of Genesis, Cain murdered his brother Abel because he felt rejected and inferior.

But if we look closer, there are other examples of people in the Bible who overcame the spirit of rejection even in extreme circumstances and rose above it to serve God in a mighty way. For example, Joseph's brothers sold him into slavery and he ended up in prison. Joseph could have rotted in prison a bitter and rejected dude, and who would blame him for those emotions? But he chose to believe God had a better plan for him, and He raised Joseph out of his circumstances to become an overseer of the land.

And nobody knows rejection better than Jesus. I remember one time after I moved to LA in my twenties when I was feeling so low and confused. I came home and cried on my bedroom floor, not knowing what God wanted to do with me. I wanted to serve Him, but I couldn't find my place. I couldn't take roles in Hollywood that were being offered, and I had been kicked out of most ministry teams because I hate manual labor.

I opened my Bible to Isaiah 53:3-4:

> He was despised and rejected by mankind,
> a man of suffering and familiar with pain.
> Like one from whom people hide their faces
> he was despised, and we held him in low esteem.
>
> Surely he took up our pain
> and bore our suffering,
> yet we considered him punished by God,
> stricken by him, and afflicted.

There on my bedroom floor my life changed. I realized that Jesus walked in the ultimate rejection and sacrifice for me and took it to the cross so I don't have to carry that stuff. He defeated Satan and all his lies so I could be free. I prayed that day, "God, use me and lead me wherever You want me to go."

I had moved out of Hollywood and settled in at the beach and connected with a great church and went to auditions when they arose. But this was the moment when God, and I mean *only God*, gave me the idea to try stand-up comedy...in Hollywood. I never would have thought of that on my own. I knew God wanted me to serve Him, but how could stand-up comedy be any kind of ministry? I believe God said, "Well, You have a big mouth and a crazy life. Show the world I can use anyone!" I ended up back in Hollywood studying stand-up comedy and doing a boot camp season in the clubs every night. I talked about my faith on stage, and guess what? It worked! People laughed. I got to pray for comics, bartenders, and even some drag queens.

If I had believed all those lies of rejection the devil wanted me to, there is no way I ever could have had the courage to take the stage in the ultimate vulnerable position...just me and a microphone. But like my mama, and the Bible, always says, "With God all things are possible!" (Matthew 19:26). That was 13 years ago, and I'm still enjoying the ride. I still have my moments of insecurity, but in those times I have to go back to the truth about me. I am fearfully and wonderfully made, and God has a destiny for me that is great.

For we are his workmanship, created in Christ Jesus for good works, which God prepared beforehand, that we should walk in them (Ephesians 2:10 ESV).

● ● ●

## TO THINK ON

- Do you struggle with rejection and feeling unworthy? How has that affected your life?
- What lies have you believed about yourself that might have held you back from living your fullest destiny?

● ● ●

*Dear God,*

*I don't want to believe any lies about myself anymore. Please help reveal what the enemy has lied to me about and cast it out of my mind. I know I am loved, accepted, and created in Your image. Thank You for the good works You have prepared in advance for me to do for Your kingdom. Thank You for choosing me, God.*

*In Jesus' name.*

*Amen.*

# IS BOTOX A SIN?

## (I Might Be in Trouble)

*I praise you, for I am fearfully and wonderfully made.*
*Wonderful are your works; my soul knows it very well.*

**PSALM 139:14 ESV**

When one of my favorite TV evangelists came under fire for having a face-lift, she said, "Well, I prayed about it and God said, 'It's your face; do what you want!'" She's in her seventies, and I'm sure is well past the point of caring about what other people think about her decisions, but she must care about the way people think she looks enough to go under the knife. Where I live in LA, people don't age; they just start to look more like they were cryogenically frozen. I always made fun of my friends for getting a little injection or filler. I had one friend who was so obsessed with her "fat" ankles she had liposuction, and then while she was there, the doctor decided to suck out the fat from her legs!

I never thought I would sell my soul enough to modify what God gave me. After all, God don't make trash! I was having some rosacea on my face and decided to go to LA's fanciest dermatologist. She is in Beverly Hills, and they practically greet you with a cappuccino or drink of choice (extra $50.00). Then Dr. Fancy Pants came in to chat. I told her I was having some issues with rosacea and she stopped me and said, "That's nice, dear, but don't you think we need to deal with the fact that the 405 freeway looks like it's running across your forehead? And what about the fact that your eye lids are uneven…"

I felt like I was on an episode of *Botched*. I didn't know whether to nod in agreement or storm out in righteous indignation. But the sun was setting over the ocean and they offered me candy and the next thing I knew, this woman was sticking a needle in my forehead! Yes, Botox! She was like a very calm, kind drug dealer whispering, "Shh... the first one's free! You're gonna love it! You want to be happy, don't you?" Maybe she didn't say those exact words, but that's what I heard in my head as the piercing pain pricked my skin.

And then guess what happened? It was like a plague from God. I started to break out in hives! Yes, full-blown hives all over my forehead! She was calling in the nurse like in an episode of *ER*, and they were shooting me up with Benadryl and taking away my Shirley Temple. I left 20 minutes later with an ice pack and a load of guilt.

As I looked at my swollen face in my car mirror, I told God I was sorry for messing up His "masterpiece." The very next morning all the hives had disappeared. I took a long, hard look at my face in the mirror and thought, *I look...amazing!* "I feel pretty, oh so pretty!" was dancing through my head. Those freeway lines had faded away, and the crinkles between my eyebrows were now smoothed to perfection. The only problem was...I couldn't move my eyebrows to express my delight. I had gained the fountain of youth and lost my facial expressions. But who needs expressions when we have emojis?

I saw my friend Suzie, whom I had previously chastised for being in the "B" club. We couldn't show our emotions with our Botoxed faces, so we hugged in delight. Maybe I'm exaggerating this story; maybe I'm not. But here's the truth: all of this happened, and I can't tell you I feel bad about it. Is that wrong?

I think it comes down to a heart issue. If I'm changing myself on the outside because I really need a makeover on the inside, I am going about it backward. I need to know that God made me beautiful from the inside out and be secure in that. If I want to do a little maintenance, I think He might be okay with it. As long as when I get to the pearly gates, Jesus doesn't take one look at me and say, "Get away from Me. I don't recognize you!"

Then I'll reply, "Hold on, Jesus. I've got some old photos I'd like to show You."

. . .

## TO THINK ON

- How do you feel about yourself on the inside and the outside?

- If you ever thought about making physical changes, what was the motivation? Did you pray about it first?

- No, seriously…check this out about the Proverbs 31 Woman: "Charm is deceptive, and beauty is fleeting; but a woman who fears the LORD is to be praised" (verse 30).

. . .

*Dear God,*

*Thank You for the examples of women to be praised in the Bible. Please help me know that my truest beauty will always start with my inner self and that the rest is just decoration. Thank You for all the words written in Your Word about how much You love me and think I am beautiful.*

*In Jesus' name.*

*Amen.*

Day 24

# BIG GIRLS DON'T CRY

*I have told you these things, so that in me you may*
*have peace. In this world you will have trouble. But*
*take heart! I have overcome the world.*

**JOHN 16:33**

When I drive my kids to school, we listen to either (a) a Christian station, (b) Broadway show tunes, or (c) '80s music. You can guess which station gets the most airtime. And it's not like I don't make it spiritual. My kids are convinced Bon Jovi was a Christian band ("Livin' on a Prayer") and George Michael could have been a Christian singer ("Ya Gotta Have Faith"). See? I can make anything Christian! I knew I was a good mom when Lucy cried the day David Bowie died, and Ruby is still sad she can't marry Prince.

Music is a powerful tool to jog memories—good, bad, and gut-wrenching. I can't get through a Journey song without tearing up just a little. One day after I dropped off my kids at school, I was driving home by the beach and it was the most perfect day of bliss. (That's why we mortgage a kidney to pay taxes to live here in La La Land.) And all of a sudden I heard those familiar violins, and then came the piano and there it was, the beginning of "I've Had the Time of My Life" from the iconic movie *Dirty Dancing*. It was the instrumental version, and I was bawling silently while driving down the Pacific Coast Highway.

No, I wasn't just mourning the loss of Patrick Swayze. You see, that was my wedding song. I married someone in show business, and our wedding was quite the epic affair. The theme was "Movie Premier," and we had a red carpet and paparazzi greeting guests, and we did our own comedic version of "the dance" and "the lift"! (If you are over the age of 30 this will make sense to you.) And the whole night was perfection. We continued to do that dance as part of our comedy act for years, including once when I was deathly ill passing a kidney stone in front of 30,000 people! Ron was always up for anything that would entertain and bring people joy. And for 12 years that's what we did. It's just that no one saw the struggles behind the scenes except a select few loved ones. Everyone else saw us living the charmed life.

Who would have predicted that I'd be driving down the road as a divorced single mom, sobbing like a baby to a bunch of violins. We had good closure. We co-parent like champs. But I didn't want to be divorced. Some days I feel as if I wrestled with Satan himself to save the marriage and lost. As the music played, all the old questions started swirling in my head: "Why couldn't it have worked?" "Why couldn't You save it, God?" "Where were You?" "Why me?" And "Why am I blubbering like an idiot years later when I thought I was over it?" I felt so stupid for crying, and I was throwing up prayers like hand grenades. My chest was so tight it literally hurt.

I never wanted to be in this position, and no matter what I did or prayed or tried, it happened anyway. And there was nothing I could do about it. It still hurt so much. I hate losing battles.

But since God has a sense of humor, just then the second song from the soundtrack came on loudly: Frankie Valli singing "Big Girls Don't Cry!"

I busted out laughing in my car. God's timing was impeccable. "Okay, touché, God! You heard me. You needed to break up the water works and You knew just how to do it." I didn't hear an audible voice of comfort from God; I heard the Four Seasons singing in my ear. Hilarious! Perfect! Just what I needed.

I know I won't ever have all the answers for why things like divorce or other life-altering events happen. We don't know the why or when hard times are going to strike.

God wasn't surprised by my divorce, and He never told me there would be an expiration date on the pain and loss. I wish there were, but

I don't know how long it's going to hurt. That's why I'm glad my time in this life is short compared to my time in the heaven. Maybe I'll get a chance to sit down with God face-to-face and ask all my nagging questions. But more than likely I'll be so overwhelmed to be in His presence that none of the pain on earth will matter anymore.

Jesus told us clearly we would face trials, but He also promised us that He was the one who could bring us peace in knowing they would come. There is something to look forward to if we put our trust in Him.

• • •

## TO THINK ON

- Serious question: What's your favorite '80s song?
- Does God ever speak to you in a particularly personal or even humorous way?

• • •

*Dear God,*

*Thank You for creating music and lyrics that speak to our souls. Thank You for having a sense of humor that is often overlooked. Thank You for speaking to me just the way You know I will hear You and making it so personal. I love You.*

*In Jesus' name.*

*Amen.*

# JUST ANOTHER MANIC MONDAY

*Remember the Sabbath day by keeping it holy. Six days you shall labor and do all your work, but the seventh day is a sabbath to the LORD your God. On it you shall not do any work.*

**EXODUS 20:8-10**

Do you ever wake up feeling blue? It's Monday, and I don't want to face it. Today I woke up and my neck ached and I had a dream about an old friend I haven't seen for years and I just don't feel like bouncing up and taking on the day. I'm way more Eeyore today than Tigger.

I feel a bit sad knowing that if I get on the scale, it will confirm that my summer of eating has taken a toll on my waistline, and I haven't seen the inside of a gym in months because my bathing suit has a nice skirt so, well, that was a good trade. I don't want to do Monday today because in one more week it will be Manic Monday: the ever-dreaded school year is starting. I'm not ready to face all the pressures of fall. And yesterday was so filled up with church activity, family visits, and a late-night concert that none of us got much sleep.

I feel a sense of dread that my mornings will become frantic races to feed these little people some type of sustenance and get them relatively presentable and into the car to fight traffic while screaming spelling words and Bible verses. I will then fill my days with work and appointments until 3:00 p.m., when we will begin the marathon of gymnastic lessons, homework battles, dinner preparation, cleanup, baths, and some semblance of devotions together before the hour-long bedtime ritual, which will include three glasses of water, last-minute bathroom trips, and night-light adjustments. After I tuck them in *again*, a huge pile of their laundry will be glaring at me, saying, "Hey, they are going to bed! Don't you need to wash me so they have uniforms tomorrow?"

I feel a bit lonely, and I suppose that's normal. Maybe I've been watching too many rom-coms and reality shows. I sometimes wish there was a partner to run this amazing race with, and if he happened to be cute and not snore, that wouldn't hurt either. I have a full life of friends and family and work, so why do I feel so empty sometimes? I have two little mouths to feed, and just thinking about all that's on my shoulders is enough to make me want to pull the covers back over my head and refuse to get out of bed for at least two days. I could fake a cold? No, because I'm a mom.

I started this day at 8:00 a.m. This morning my kids ate a loaf of bread with butter for breakfast and snacked on Popsicles, corn on the cob, and juice boxes. I ended up doing a mom/daughter devotion with Lucy and then I took them swimming at my neighbor Bronwyn's house, where we sat and sipped kombucha (which she made) and I watched her grill salmon and pretended to help. Then I came home and let them play games while we snacked on mango and melon. Now we're going to watch a movie, and I'm sure we'll watch *The Golden Girls* as our nightly tradition to fall asleep, which has continued all summer.

It was a glorious day, and I really didn't get much done at all. I definitely didn't get any work done. I didn't spend hours in prayer, but I did have some time with my daughter to commune with God. I think God was very much a part of my day because He loves me and loves to see me relaxed. I really do feel happy, and it didn't take much more than some chill time with my kids, a pool, a friend, and a fresh loaf of bread. See? Carbs make us happy! I'm not really good at taking time off to experience the joy of being with my kids. It was awesome.

I know God believes in us taking a sabbath, but I've never officially done it. However, I see how important the concept is and why God wants us to take a break. Unfortunately, our Sundays can be filled with church, brunch, sports, and even more activities than the rest of the week. No wonder we hate Mondays. We're exhausted!

God Himself rested on the seventh day. Why do we think we don't need to rest? Do we think we're stronger than God? We run on both engines until we hit a burnout point and then are forced to stop. I don't want to wait till I'm sick to actually take some time to relax and enjoy life. We need to rest, but it's not a punishment; it's a gift!

Today was a beautiful sabbath type of day, and I'm ready to take on tomorrow. Nobody ever wrote a song about crazy Tuesday!

• • •

## TO THINK ON

- When was the last time you had the luxury of a totally chill day?

- Does that sound like a pipe dream?

- How about planning a chill night or afternoon? What would you do?

• • •

*Dear God,*

*You created the Sabbath for a reason and I see why. Please help me find a way to sabbath because it's good for my mind, body, and soul. Thank You for knowing what is best for me emotionally, spiritually, and physically. Help me learn to rest.*

*In Jesus' name.*

*Amen.*

# IS THERE A POWER OUTAGE IN HEAVEN?

*Whatever you ask in my name, this I will do, that*
*the Father may be glorified in the Son. If you*
*ask me anything in my name, I will do it.*

**JOHN 14:13-14 ESV**

D o you ever find yourself praying a prayer like this: "Oh God, please heal my neck and back and headache? Especially my neck, that's the worst. If You can only heal one thing, would You…"

Or what about this: "Dear Lord, sorry to bother You, but I just have this favor to ask…"

Are we praying like there is going to be a power outage in heaven if we ask for too much? Do we think God is too busy to handle all of our prayer requests? When Jesus healed the lepers, did He heal most of their body but leave one arm all messed up? No! And didn't Jesus say we would have all power and authority that He had through the Holy Spirit after He left the earth?

Where did we come up with the idea that we need to give God a list of wants and then prioritize which ones for Him to do first? Do we think He's like Santa and we have to make a Christmas list like we did when we were kids? Put a star by the things we want most? God wants to hear all of our prayers and He doesn't put them on some sort of list in order of importance. The Bible says, "You do not have because you do not ask God" (James 4:2).

I know our prayer list of needs can seem long and overwhelming at times. Sometimes I just pray in earnest, "Fix it, God! All of it! I need You!" When I can't muster the words to explain all my sorrows and hurts, I can still call out to Him and He knows my heart and exactly what I need. Prayer is not meant to be like going before a king or a judge solely to grant our petitions. Prayer is meant to deepen a real relationship with a God who created us, put us on this planet at this particular time in history, and knew exactly what we were going to face every single day. And the best part? He also knows exactly how we are going to overcome each obstacle that we are dealt and how He is going to help us. He's a loving Father and longs for us to see Him that way.

My kids have a favorite word, and it has many meanings. It's *Mom*! That word could be spoken lovingly and gently or screamed from the backyard—"Mooooommmm!" But they know either way, Mom is going to respond and help sort out the situation. Maybe I need to officiate a fight over Barbies or kiss a boo-boo or hug a crying child. No matter what, I'm going to do whatever I can to make it better for my children.

Some needs are small; others are of epic proportions because somebody decided to try to fly like Wonder Woman off the couch and skinned both knees. Would I ever get them a Band-Aid for one knee and let the other one bleed because I ran out of Band-Aids? Hello? Moms are *never* short on Band-Aids! And God is never short on love and blessings for us. We just have to stop being scared to ask for what we want.

My children have *no* problem asking me for everything at once. They know Mom can handle it. Now, I'm only human and I do the best I can. But can you imagine how much more our heavenly Father can do to comfort us, guide us, and even heal us when the needs arise?

What about praying about our hopes and dreams? Do we have the courage to include God in something so big we haven't even told anyone about it? I hope so, because I think God wants to be included in every part of our journey. And when the dreams come true, we can tell others that God is a good God of blessings. He's not human. He won't make fun of our dreams; in fact, He's the one who created us to dream.

God likes to do things big. Just look at the way He has rescued His people miraculously or the incredible miracles He's performed. Take a look at your own life and remind yourself of how He has provided for you and blessed you.

One of my favorite quotes from the great philosopher Willie Wonka is: "We are the music makers, and we are the dreamers of dreams." God created us each with unique desires and dreams, and we shouldn't be afraid to go to Him about them. After all, He parted the Red Sea. He can help you lose that ten pounds you've been trying to shed for the last three years or help you achieve that secret goal nobody knows about. Trust Him. Talk to Him. He won't let you down! Just remember to give Him the glory.

. . .

## TO THINK ON

- Do you ever pray partial prayers?
- Is there an area in your life you've been afraid to ask God about because it seems too big?
- Can you stretch your faith to believe and ask for more?

. . .

*Dear God,*

*Forgive me for my tiny faith sometimes. Forgive me for not trusting that You can handle all of my problems, hopes, and desires at once because You are an all-knowing, all-loving God. Help me stretch my faith and continue to see You working out every detail in my life. There is no prayer too big or too small for You.*

*In Jesus' name.*

*Amen.*

Day 27

# FITBIT IN CHURCH

## (She's a Maniac...Maniac...in the Pew!)

*Therefore, since we are surrounded by so great a cloud*
*of witnesses, let us also lay aside every weight, and*
*sin which clings so closely, and let us run with*
*endurance the race that is set before us, looking to*
*Jesus, the founder and perfecter of our faith.*
**HEBREWS 12:1-2 ESV**

If there is one predictable trait about me, it's that I like to win. I'm not quite as vicious as my mother (God bless her) or as ruthless as my brother, but I have a pretty intense competitive streak. Don't play board games with my family unless you want to meet the cops. I was always the kid in school who finished every test early. Back then, getting answers right wasn't as important as the feeling of being first.

Being competitive isn't all bad. It helps me accomplish goals and survive in the blood-bath I call Hollywood. We're competing whether we like to or not every time we audition. I'm mellowing out lately, but it's still a struggle—I won't lie.

My latest endeavor involves this little thing called a Fitbit. It wraps around your wrist and tracks your steps throughout the day like Big Brother. It's supposed to help me lose weight. (Cutting back on my nightly s'mores might also be a solid choice as well.) But since I *love* food, I chose the Fitbit.

You set a goal and try to get as many steps in as possible. For a type A person like me, this plan can work to my advantage. But sometimes my competitiveness rears its ugly head and it's…well, not pretty! A good example of this problem happened at church last week.

I was doing my praise and worship time and, as previously mentioned, my church is very active. We stand up and sing and move around as we feel led and always have a great time. I glanced down at my Fitbit and noticed that every time I danced a little, that number was moving upward toward my goal! I thought, *If I get a good dose of the Spirit, I can jog in place and nobody will notice.* So the next thing you know, I'm jogging and waving my hands in the air like I'm on fire…for Jesus!

Need a visual? Think *Flashdance*! (Millennials, google that.)

I was pretty stoked to get in my extra steps and appear a little extra spiritual in front of my peers (who were not watching, by the way; they were too busy droppin' it like it's hot!). I could picture God laughing at me in heaven. I must have appeared insane from His view to be concentrating so hard on winning when there was no one to compete against. I was focusing on shaping up physically, not feeding my spirit. I missed the point completely. I have a lot of work to do in this area.

I'm reading the Bible in one year, and I caught myself racing through Leviticus just to keep on track. I'm currently a month behind, and it bothers me daily. But am I reading God's Word to take it in or am I just trying to win? And win what? A prize? Bragging rights? Nobody cares how fast I read my Bible. It's just me and the competition I've created in my pretty little head. When behavior borders on ridiculous, I think it's time to take a step back and reevaluate our spiritual life and ask who we are competing with and what is taking away from our organic experience.

Take, for example, reading my Bible in a year. Now I do my best to get through the day's reading, but I'm trying to focus on all the things I'm learning. Before I hadn't spent a lot of time reading all the details of what the Israelites went through. But now, after reading through the Old Testament, when I study about Israel's current struggle and see all the opposition they've faced through the centuries, it makes more sense to me. I have more of a heart to pray for Israel and support the efforts going on there.

I don't want to miss what God wants me to see from His Word by trying to win some fictional prize for being fast. This isn't vacation Bible school, and God isn't passing out ribbons and Popsicles (even though those would be nice). He's passing out knowledge and wisdom and the supernatural lessons that come from the Holy Spirit. There are *no* shortcuts to learning these lessons.

I'm really enjoying this year-in-the-Bible experience and hopefully growing in my relationship with God. I don't want to shortchange God or get shortchanged myself by rushing because there really isn't a finish line until we get to heaven. For now, I'll do my best to focus on each task at hand while trying not to be a super multitasker when no one asked me to. The prize is in the journey.

• • •

## TO THINK ON

- Have you ever tried to multitask with less than stellar results?
- Do you find yourself struggling to be in the moment when it comes to your relationship with God?

• • •

*Dear Lord,*

*You gave me this brain, and I'm grateful for all it does to help me. When this brain is going in too many directions, I ask that You help me focus and slow down. Only You can help me, God. I need You. I don't want to miss anything You have for me.*

*In Jesus' name.*

*Amen.*

# DIFFERENT, YET THE SAME

*You made all the delicate, inner parts of my body
and knit me together in my mother's womb.
Thank you for making me so wonderfully complex!
Your workmanship is marvelous—how well I know it.*

**PSALM 139:13-14 NLT**

To all the moms out there who wrap their six-year-olds in baby blankets because you know it's your last child, this is for you.

I get it now. We put forth so much effort pushing our firstborn to walk and talk and do algebra before preschool that by the time the second one comes along, we're exhausted from trying to get our first child into Harvard early admission before they go to first grade.

I gave birth to a gifted, overachieving firstborn child who now, at age ten, is absolutely convinced she has no need of me. When she was nine months old, she insisted she didn't need to breastfeed anymore. Just recently she informed us that she's going to live with her grandparents or go to New York City this summer. Of course it was with great thrill that we watched her hit every milestone early, and I happily reported each effort to everyone on social media. And when she was two, I decided I'd like to give birth next time to a child who would like me.

Things were different from the very start with Ruby. She has a very different personality, and I love it. Whereas Lucy will look at a slide and think it will help her fly, Ruby will get up on the top and spend ten minutes figuring out if this way down is too scary or not. Ruby is cautious and careful, and Lucy is carefree and crazy. God knew I needed both of these minions to make my life complete.

I've actually relished having a child who needs me. It's never been a burden as she reaches for my leg in a crowded store or still asks me to help her peel a Fruit Roll-Up. I love when she calls me Mama.

It's going too fast. And as much as I love them, they each have their own particular and special way of driving me bananas. It's like they were both equipped with this superpower at birth.

Sometimes my little one has bad dreams, so I need to check on her after she falls asleep. I went to look in on her as she slept tonight and noticed her whole body is getting longer. I didn't see this coming; it snuck up on me. I wrapped her in a baby blanket and took her over to the rocking chair. These days my best cuddles happen while she's sleeping. I rocked her and told her very softly, "My darling little Ruby Joy, you are not allowed to get any bigger or older, for Mommy is fearful that you will need her less. Do you hear me? I am not allowing it. You must always be able to fit in my lap right here in this chair."

At that moment my fearless, flying ten-year-old woke up and saw me singing to her sister. She sleepily climbed up into my arms and said, "Rock me, Mama!" I realized there is still a part of Lucy that will always be my baby. There I was, trying to balance two children in my lap without letting them know I was in excruciating pain. The most precious moments sometimes come with a little bittersweet pain. But as long as my kids want to cuddle in my lap, even if they are 16, I'm going to make it work! (I wonder if that would work with my mom?)

I appreciate that my daughters are completely different, but they both need me. I bet that's how God feels about all His children. We are so unique in the most wonderful ways. But at the core of who we are, we are His children and we *all* need Him, whether we know it or not.

It must break His heart to see His children running amuck just as the Israelites did in the Bible. Seems like the minute Moses went up that mountain, they were making that golden calf as an idol. I bet God was thinking, *You kids. I can't even turn My back for one minute, and you all are getting into trouble!*

But every time they said they were sorry, God was there in a heartbeat to rescue them from all evil. Did God cause the evil? No! But God was ready to forgive and forget, and I'm glad He hasn't changed. It must have been so bittersweet to see all the pain His children caused themselves by turning their backs on Him. But when they came running back to His arms, I bet it was a glorious moment because, as He said, "As far as the east is from the west, so far has he removed our transgressions from us" (Psalm 103:12).

He is the best dad because He literally remembers our sins no more. I wonder if those sins include making funnel cakes without permission?

• • •

## TO THINK ON

- When you read about God's children turning their back on Him so many times in the Bible, do you relate to them?
- How do you think God feels when you've gone astray from Him?
- Do you feel He has willing arms to welcome you back?

• • •

*Dear God,*

*Thank You for making me like no one else. Thank You that I'm a unique creation made in Your likeness. Please forgive me when I act exactly like Your children in the Bible who broke Your heart. Sometimes the world can sway me away from You and I don't even see it happening. I'm so very grateful You are there to welcome me back into Your arms every single time I'm sorry. I love You.*

*In Jesus' name.*

*Amen.*

# HANGRY

## Yes, It's a Thing

*Jesus said to them, "I am the bread of life;
he who comes to Me will not hunger, and he
who believes in Me will never thirst."*

**JOHN 6:35 NASB**

woke up this fine Saturday morning with all sorts of gusto. I even put my Bible reading on audio as a brushed my teeth because, well, I'm super Christian. I got through almost two days of Hosea when my youngest daughter, Ruby, got up asking to watch *The Muppets*. I knew I would have plenty of time to do my full devotions this morning and start my day off right after I helped her blow her runny nose and situated her in front of the TV with frozen bananas for breakfast.

Well, before that happened I discovered I would have to do the same load of laundry a third time because I kept forgetting to put it in the dryer. Then I noticed how unorganized my garage was so I started moving suitcases around until I heard noises in my kitchen and smelled smoke. Chef Lucy had woken up and decided to make omelets. She had never made omelets, much less breakfast before, unless you count Fruity Pebbles and a cupcake on my birthday.

I walked into the kitchen and it looked like a crime scene. Her version of an omelet was to put eggs in the pan and then sprinkle every single spice we have on it, including black pepper and dill weed. Egg shells were everywhere, and my spice rack that I had meticulously organized was in complete disarray. She offered me a bite and I told her, "Mommy is fasting," because my ex-husband just lost 50 pounds by not eating breakfast. I decided today was a good day to start that diet. #intermittent-fasting

Instead of eating I decided to get out that three-ring recipe binder and consider cooking sometime this week, but really I just wanted to look at pictures of food. My stomach was growling.

Then I realized Ruby's tutor was coming. It was the tutor's birthday, so we had to tape up her sign and put out the balloons. As I was looking for the balloons, I heard a loud popping sound in my living room. Lucy had found my polka dot balloons and decided to make stress balls by filling them with Elmer's Glue. She was covered in glue, and so was my floor. Did I mention Lucy was dressed up because we needed to tape her acting audition to play Meryl Streep's granddaughter?

So my living room and kitchen were both trashed and it was 10:00 a.m. I then saw that Ruby had taken frozen watermelon when I wasn't looking and eaten it on my couch and dripped the fruit juice all over my shabby chic comforter that is on my couch to cover all the other stains. I had to strip the couch and rearrange all the pillows.

As I was returning the pillows to the linen closet I saw that it was in shambles. So I took out every single pillowcase, sheet, and blanket and refolded them, knowing this would last about 48 hours until someone pulled them all out again to build a fort. And why do I still have baby blankets?

I definitely thought about doing my devotions and headed to my bedroom to do just that, but I saw the kitchen hadn't been cleaned, even though I specifically told Lucy to wipe off the counter and put the dishes in the dishwasher. I called Lucy in my kindest drill sergeant voice and went off on her way too long about her lack of cleaning skills and told her that her chef days were over. I also decided she didn't do enough chores and we needed to make a chore chart immediately.

Then I saw their room and had to call in Ruby to yell at her about the disorganization of her shoes and the amount of stuffed animals she had under her bed along with candy wrappers and empty boxes of raisins. I was losing it. I was saying things to a child like, "You're a hoarder! How can you live like this?" It was bad.

I was feeling like a grouch. Then it was like God spoke to me: "You haven't fed yourself, My darling, in any way!" I was *hangry*! I had heard about this term for being hungry and angry, but until this moment I didn't know it was real.

All of those activities could have been handled with much more peace and sanity if I had had a full belly and a fed soul. But in the battle of the wills, the sneaky devil had won again. Okay, let's be honest. This was all me! I can't blame him. He didn't have to try that hard. I got on the hamster wheel all by myself...again.

I did finally get to read my Bible, and it was good. So was the plate of fried rice and Korean food I scarfed down. If I learned one thing today, it's that it's good to be fed in every area. If I am not in God's Word, I feel starved. It doesn't happen right away, but I will feel like something is off in my life. I wish I picked up on the subtle or not-so-subtle cues more quickly. I find myself becoming short-tempered and anxious. And after running to all of my usual vices—sugar, social media, and friends—I realize that when Jesus said, "I am the bread of life," He wasn't kidding. He gave us His Word to live on, and we need it every day just as much as we need avocado toast and fried rice, if not more.

• • •

## TO THINK ON

- Have you ever been hangry? How did you handle it?
- What are you doing in your daily life to feed your soul?
- How can you spiritually feed yourself more consistently in your daily life?

• • •

*Dear God,*

*You created food and Your Word for my nourishment. I doubt it's a good idea to skip either of those things. I'm sorry if I got off track today, and I appreciate You still being there when I came to my senses. Thanks for inventing all different ways for me to feed my soul. Help me use them.*

*In Jesus' name.*

*Amen.*

# CAN GOD SPEAK THROUGH BOB MARLEY?

*My sheep listen to my voice; I know them, and they*
*follow me. I give them eternal life, and they shall never*
*perish; no one will snatch them out of my hand.*

**JOHN 10:27-28**

was having one of those no good, very bad, terrible days the other day. It's not worth telling you all my worries, woes, and everything that was going wrong. We'd need two books! But I couldn't snap out of it, no matter what I tried. You know, the kind of day where you go out and buy Ben and Jerry's for therapeutic purposes and it still doesn't make you feel better. I washed down the ice cream with Coca-Cola, and all I felt was bloated and guilty. I love food, but unfortunately it does not solve all my problems the way I think it will. This day was filled with so much uncertainty mixed with bad news, and I didn't know where to turn. We all have days like this, don't we?

I was driving in my car and trying to hold it together because I had to pick up my kids. But the tears just wouldn't stay inside my eye sockets! And then a song came on the radio and the singer had a soothing, familiar voice that almost sounded like God speaking to me, if God had a Rastafarian accent and played some mean reggae drum and bass.

"No woman, no cry!" His smooth tones transported me to a faraway beach where the ocean breezes blew in my sun-soaked face and I didn't have a care in the world because I knew everything was "gonna be all right"!

Okay, so was God speaking to me through Bob Marley? I mean,

it happens in movies. Why couldn't it happen in my car? I wiped the tears away and listened to the words and pretended it was God putting His huge arms around me and literally telling me, "Don't cry… everything's gonna be all right!" And you know what? I did my best to listen, and I felt a bit better. I'm not going to tell you all my worries went away, but as I listened to the beautiful music, I chose to relax a bit and once again remember God is in control.

I picked up the girls and came home and got them changed and ready for another one of the free food festivals we've been attending this summer. This one was downtown, and all the eateries were giving out samples in Caribbean tropical style.

At the end of the night there was a live calypso band playing. I walked up to hear the melodious sounds, and guess what words were drifting out over the sunset?

"No woman, no cry."

My youngest daughter grabbed my hand and started dancing with me and twirling. The sun was setting. Our bellies were full of free treats, and all my cares seemed to float away, even if it was just for one night. I danced with my daughters in the warm summer night. And I was overwhelmed with how much God must love me to work so hard to get such a simple message through my head. He even sent an entire calypso band to make sure I got the point. I'm telling you, I can't make this stuff up! God can definitely speak through music…even Bob Marley! God created me to love music. It's a love language of mine. And that's how He knows He can get through to my hurting heart.

• • •

## TO THINK ON

- Take a moment to think of a special way God speaks to you that's just between the two of you.

- Have you ever had a music moment where you felt as though God was speaking directly to you?

- How did it make you feel?

• • •

*Dear God,*

*I can't believe the lengths You will go to show me how much You love me. Thank You for creating music in all shapes and forms that speak directly to my heart. You are the maker of all good things. I'm grateful.*

*In Jesus' name.*

*Amen.*

Day 31

# THE PURGE

*I am the vine; you are the branches. If you
remain in me and I in you, you will bear much
fruit; apart from me you can do nothing.*

**JOHN 15:5**

Okay, call me a bad mom. But I just got through going through my kids playroom and getting rid of things...a lot of things. They have too much stuff, and I don't want to end up on an episode of *Hoarders*. Does my child really need every school paper she has ever completed? Any toy that even resembles something from a fast food drive through was out! I think the playroom was getting so out of control my kids didn't even know how to find any of their toys and that's why my youngest has been running around the house with a piece of wood like it's a sword pretending she's Joan of Arc. I've spent hundreds of dollars on expensive toys, and she's most happy with a piece of wood. Irony!

I love to purge. It feels great, and nothing brings me more joy than clearing out junk and discovering a new use for space, whether it's my garage shelves or clothes closets. I'm really trying to live in a "less is more" way. I keep telling myself, "Be a minimalist! Be a minimalist! It's a better way to live!" It gives me clarity and peace to have more space in my space.

Now, my kids are usually clueless when I ransack their playroom and never ask me where a missing plastic toy is or where their broken Barbie disappeared to. By the way, I hate naked Barbies. If she's nude, she's out, especially if she has one leg. Are my kids savages or what? But if they happen to see I'm throwing out something, that particular item becomes their most cherished item of all time. Bring on the tears! Even if it hasn't been played with in months and they don't even know where it came from, they can't bear to part with it whatever "it" is.

I have to do this type of purging for myself too because I have a nasty habit of acquiring things. I am never one to say no to hand-me-downs or garage sale finds. I love the art of the hunt, and whether I specifically need it or not does not stop me from purchasing or accepting it. I'm exactly like my kids, but at least I'm a bit more aware when things are piling up around me. Or am I?

I got to thinking today as I was making my thirteenth trip to the recycling bin, *How does God feel about my life? What is piling up around me? What would God like to purge out of my life if I gave Him permission?* I know we've all heard of the lofty prayer, "Lord, prune me and take what is not pleasing to You." Have you prayed that prayer like I have and then grimaced and ducked to see what God was going to grab? It's one of the scariest prayers you could ever pray if you mean it.

Would you let God purge some of your things and possibly even relationships that are becoming unhealthy for you? Do you trust Him to do that in your life with love and care, even though it could hurt for a minute? We cling to things and people and habits like my kids cling to an unusable tangled slinky or an airplane with no wings.

I can't tell you the number of past relationships God purged for me and later I realized I'd dodged a bullet. God could see the outcome wasn't going to be pretty, and I'm eternally grateful He was gracious enough to yank me out of the pot of simmering, slow-boiling water I was hanging out in. This goes for bad habits, bad living situations, bad jobs, and other clutter in my life I needed to purge but I had been blinded because I had become comfortable in my own mess. Some of these things were starting to rot, and they had to go immediately before they started to smell.

God has a better view of my life than I do, and I've learned to trust and believe that when He helps me (sometimes a bit painfully) let go of something, there is a good reason. I may not know why I've lost some things this side of heaven. But there are enough times He's bailed me out that His track record is pretty solid.

I still pray that prayer—"Prune what needs to go in my life"—with one eye open. But I know when He's at work it's going to produce better fruit in my life in the long run. I don't want to be a branch with sour grapes or a naked Barbie with one leg. And I want to set an example of trusting God for my kids.

I thought I had made progress as a mom one Christmas when I saw my sweet five-year-old Lucy loading toys into a plastic bag. I said, "Oh, honey, what are you doing?" She replied, "I'm giving these toys to the orphans." I was so proud and said, "That's amazing. What prompted you to do this?" She said completely straight-faced, "So I can get off the naughty list for Santa!" #motherhoodcrushingit

• • •

## TO THINK ON

- Is there any commitment, relationship, or situation in your life that needs purging?
- Where are you feeling cluttered in your life? Is it physical or emotional clutter?

• • •

*Dear Lord,*

*I don't want to be a hoarder in any area of my life, but I'm scared of what You will say needs to go. Please help me purge, but be gentle as only You can. It's not easy for me to pray this prayer.*

*In Jesus' name.*

*Amen.*

Day 32

# VIRTUAL REALITY CHECK

*What good is it for someone to gain the whole
world, and yet lose or forfeit their very self?*

**LUKE 9:25**

If a tree falls in the forest and no one took a selfie with it, did it fall? If
I take my kids to the beach and don't talk about it on Facebook, does
it count? We are living in this overly documented world where even
the foods we eat for breakfast are fodder for loved ones and strangers
to debate. I love/hate my relationship with social media. I love making
people laugh with my posts, but I hate that it has become addicting.

I went to a carnival with my kids yesterday. I was standing in the hot
sun waiting for a ride with Ruby, and I looked around to see every single parent either on their phones or snapping photos and posting. Can't
we actually enjoy a moment without having to be photographic journal-
ists? Can we just *be* without constantly reaching for our pocket technology to entertain us? Have you ever looked at a bus station and noticed
that absolutely nobody is making eye contact with anyone else because
their heads are buried in their phones? You want to know a secret? Guess
what I was doing that day at the carnival? I'll give you one guess…*click,
click, snap, snap.* #Instaperfect #motherhoodcrushingit #Sundayfunday

I know I'm part of the problem. I could rationalize being on my
phone because I was bored standing in line and looking at it was an
easy distraction. But my daughter didn't have a phone to distract her
and she didn't seem to mind. Was she not good enough company for
me to engage her in conversation while we waited? Moments earlier I

had been playing with her and put my sunglasses on her. When I saw how adorable she looked, I just had to snap a photo for all the world to see. I couldn't just record this in my mind as a good old-fashioned memory; I needed technology to solidify that this cuteness actually occurred. And then I found myself going down the rabbit hole, checking email, responding to texts.

Gone are the days of storytelling over the dinner table. We can just say to Grandma, "Check my feed and see what the kids are up to." Friends from junior high, whom I haven't seen in over 20 years, are now privileged enough to live my life (my very filtered life) with me. And not only that, they are pressured to participate by pressing "Like" or run the risk of appearing rude.

Who created this system? Thank you, Mark Zuckerberg. I love and hate you. I suppose I'm happy for all the virtual reunions that have happened because of social media. But I can tell you I truly am ashamed of my behavior yesterday. I cared more about what thousands of strangers thought about my Sunday afternoon activities than my own daughter.

I know you might be thinking I'm overreacting. And there is nothing wrong with snapping a picture to commemorate something special. But with the onslaught of social media, is anything special anymore? I've seen strangers get engaged, volcanoes erupting, and cats playing poker, all in one 30-second scroll. Nothing really catches my attention anymore because I've seen it all. But there I was, playing the game that everyone's playing for fear I might miss out on something. You know what I was missing? Spending a fun day with my kids at a carnival, riding roller coasters, screaming, laughing, talking, and eating junk food.

Why did I need to share that for all the world to see? I really don't know the answer. Maybe I've bought into the system, but I'm starting to realize it's not healthy.

This isn't just about me as a mom; it's about me as a person who feels the need to be validated by other people more than the ones I care about most. But what am I going to do about it? I can't tell you exactly how I can fix it completely. But when I stop and see my actions are out of balance, it's up to me to do something. I took the social media apps off my phone this morning and decided to take a break. Interestingly enough, I ended up searching Amazon, Groupon, and Google News instead of Facebook. So maybe my addiction is deeper than I thought. But the good news is that I'm aware of things and can try to take control before it gets more out of hand.

I was reading my Bible today and a picture of Gwyneth Paltrow's kids popped up on my phone, which triggered me on a rabbit trail of looking at all her summer activities. I guess I'm not so different from the people I was reading about like David and Solomon. David was quite distracted by his neighbor Bathsheba, and we all know how that ended. Solomon had everything under the sun and was the wisest man in the world, but he disobeyed God and later realized the futility of a life apart from Him. So times may have changed, but God's children and our human nature haven't. But I'm glad I have the Holy Spirit guiding me in my everyday life because it's that still, small voice that makes me realize when something isn't Insta-perfect and helps me figure out how to repent to God and make it right again.

If you relate to my struggle with technology or anything else in life that seems to be more harm than good, it's not too late to change things up and live in the real unfiltered, hot-mess moments of life. They are truly the best!

P.S. I'm glad all the stupid stuff I did in college was before anyone was there to post about it! #ThankYouJesus

• • •

## TO THINK ON

- How is your relationship with technology?
- On a scale of 1 to 10, 10 being the most out of balance, where do you rate yourself?

• • •

*Dear God,*

*Some things that seem so innocent can be so harmful. Thank You for giving me foresight to see a problem mounting before it got too damaging. Please help me find proper boundaries in my social media activities.*

*In Jesus' name.*

*Amen.*

# MINI-MEAN GIRLS

*Sin is not ended by multiplying words,*
*but the prudent hold their tongues.*

**PROVERBS 10:19**

Lucy has always wanted to be a part of a certain girls organization. She loved everything about what they represent. She found out if she was a member she could even earn a college scholarship. I finally let her join a chapter, and she was over the moon. Today was her first day to meet her chapter mates and the other moms on a field trip. Lucy was so excited she even borrowed the group's handbook from a friend and was reading up on their codes and activities. I was just worried about all the cookies she would be forced to sell. I said to her dad, "You know she's going to have to sell 100 boxes of cookies!" to which he replied, "We can eat that!"

I was thrilled that this field trip was to CBS studios for a live taping of the show *So You Think You Can Dance*. When we met up with the group we exchanged polite greetings. Lucy tried to say hello to the girls but was met with awkward stares. One mom said, "Girls, give Lucy the official handshake. She's new." So they did, smiled at her a bit, and then...silence.

Lucy is a strong kid. As the tour began, she even whispered, "Mom, it can be awkward at first. I'll be okay." Then we got led backstage and were offered free unlimited snacks from the craft service table. I grabbed a bunch of stuff and loaded up my mom purse.

I am not making this up when I tell you my daughter was being completely ignored. These girls were laughing and giggling in their studio seats, and I saw Lucy on several occasions try to tap one of them on the shoulder and make conversation, to no avail. The leader mom saw what was going on and tried to nudge her daughter to engage Lucy in some type of conversation. I saw Lucy getting more upset, and I was right behind her in the row with the moms. I was sort of being ignored too, but I have a phone with internet. I didn't really care.

The leader mom said, "Well, I guess Lucy is just going to have to figure these girls out, huh?" with an awkward laugh. We asked a girl to switch seats with Lucy so she could be more in the middle. Then the girls just ignored her from both directions. Now my daughter and I were both being ignored, but I had a purse full of snacks and she didn't. I offered Lucy some candy, and my blood started to boil when I saw my daughter's face filled with disappointment and rejection. I know this feeling all too well, and it was quite painful to watch history repeat itself. I felt helpless. God was telling me to hold my tongue and I believe we've already established that is *not* my strong suit

The situation never improved, and after the show the girls kept taking selfies and walking arm in arm without my daughter. Nobody said anything, so I grabbed Lucy's arm and walked to our car after polite goodbyes. I told her, "That was not about you! And they were just mean girls. Don't take it personally. I know how you feel." "Really?" she asked "How?" as she was eating the ice cream cone I bought her. I replied, "Girl, you don't know how bad it was in 1989! It was brutal!"

We sat in the car, and I saw the tears well up in her eyes. I'm Italian and a mom. I wanted to take some un-Christian actions, but I refrained. I didn't know why this happened and why the other moms didn't do much to stop it. I was fuming inside. I wonder if the Proverbs 31 Woman was ever so mad that someone was being unkind to her kids that she wanted to jump off her camel and throw down. I had to keep my emotions in check, but it was an act of sheer will power.

I told Lucy this was a good lesson. Life is not always fair, and people are not always going to be nice and welcoming. We have to forgive them and know we will always be kind to newcomers because we know how this moment feels.

The saddest part was when Lucy said, "Mom, their code says, 'I will try to serve God and others and be considerate and caring.'" I had to explain to her that sometimes people don't keep their promises or follow the rules, and we have to forgive them anyway. I said all the right words, but I had to control my own bubbling anger and not text this leader something I'd regret. Lesson to Kerri: just because you think it doesn't mean you have to text it!

I know I can't be there to save my kids from all their heartaches, but on this occasion I did call the organization and got us assigned to a new group.

I'd do anything to help my daughter, and I know this is how God feels about all of us.

That was months ago, and my daughter is now in the most wonderful group of loving, kind girls and moms. We could not be happier. I'm so glad I made that change. I know the Holy Spirit nudged me that day. It's always a good idea to listen to that still, small voice inside of us. It can make a world of difference.

• • •

## TO THINK ON

- How do you handle gaining control of your emotions when you are hurt or angry?
- Do you sometimes act before you should and then regret it?
- How can you remind yourself to take a breath and pray first next time to have more control?

• • •

*Dear God,*

*Thank You for sending Your Holy Spirit to speak to me. The next time I feel out of control and my emotions are trying to get the best of me, help me remember to stop, drop, and pray!*

*In Jesus' name.*

*Amen.*

Day 34

# BOUNCING BALLS AND OTHER RANDOM ACTS OF KINDNESS

*So I recommend the enjoyment of life,
for there is nothing better on earth for a person to do except to
eat, drink, and enjoy life. So joy will accompany him in his toil
during the days of his life which God gives him on earth.*

**ECCLESIASTES 8:15 NET**

Sometimes I feel like I can learn more from a child about my spiritual walk than I can from a million sermons and books. (Not to badmouth books. Um…you bought mine! Thank you.) My little one, Ruby, came home with her Bible test a little while ago and she got an A. I was so proud of her, but I must admit, her handwriting looks like a doctor's or a serial killer's. I was trying to read her answers, and the last one looked as though it were written in original Hebrew. The question stated, "Tell about a time when someone showed God's love to you."

I called her over and asked her what she wrote. I needed a translation. She read, "'Mom bounces the ball with me at my house.'"

I said, "Ruby? What are you talking about? And how is a bouncing a ball representing God's love?"

"Mom, when you play ball with me, you show how you love me. I love to play with you and bounce the basketball," she answered.

My heart swelled, and I tried to hold back some sappy, emotional outburst. Ruby looked at me the way she has many times before and said, "Mom, are you crying again?"

Three days earlier I had been in between three loads of laundry and pretending to care about what Ruby was doing on my driveway. Maybe she was rigging another time machine with a cardboard box and a skateboard or maybe she was doing a jump rope marathon.

Lucy had gone to play with her friends and Ruby was happily dribbling her basketball and calling my name as she had so many times before, repeating, "Mommy, will you play with me?"

Let me be brutally honest: most of the time the answer to that question at 4:45 on a weekday would be, "No, honey, I can't right now. I have to clean and make dinner and you need to start your homework and then we will rush around the house until I tuck you in and spend ten minutes of quality time with you in your bed and leave." That's the reality.

But this day I said, "Sure, let's bounce the ball together." We played different games and laughed and had fun. Okay, I admit it, I actually enjoyed myself. When Ruby laughs, my whole world lights up.

It only lasted a short while, and then I went back to my chores. I had no idea the impact that small act of kindness would have on my child. When I heard what she had written, I was touched and then convicted. Maybe I needed to do less cleaning and more ball bouncing. Maybe the dishes can wait, or better yet, we can eat on paper plates so we'll have more playtime together as a family.

I also thought about my relationship with God. He is pleased when I stop what I'm doing to be with Him. I don't always have to be in full warfare mode, praying with some agenda. Sometimes God wants me to spiritually bounce the ball with Him and tell Him about my day. I'm not great at that because there always seem to be battles to fight. But there needs to be balance, and I need to commune with my Father God in a lighter way because it's good for my soul, body, and mind. God created us to crave connection with Him and those around us. The enemy is the one throwing in distractions.

Who in your life would be blessed just to hear from you? Is there anyone you might reach out to or maybe there's someone under your own roof who needs some time with you? Anyone you want to call? What about planning a playdate with your loved ones and you put down all chores, to-do lists, and obligations for a little while? My kids and I like to have dance parties in our living room. It might be worship music, or it might be hip-hop. I know when I'm rocking out with wild abandon it makes God smile. And my kids are all for it. As long as I don't bust a move in Costco. I gotta go…I think I hear my song!

· · ·

## TO THINK ON

- When is the last time you "bounced a ball" with someone who loves to spend time with you?
- What does spending time with God look like for you if you have a no-agenda day? Is it listening to music? Is it talking to Him about your day?

· · ·

*Dear God,*

*Please help me slow down enough to really engage with you. I don't have to be in warrior mode every time I pray. I want to learn to just be with You and have a closer relationship with You. I love You.*

*In Jesus' name,*

*Amen.*

# FUNERAL FOODS AND OTHER BAD CHOICES

*No one can serve two masters, for either he will*
*hate the one and love the other, or he will be*
*devoted to the one and despise the other.*

**MATTHEW 6:24 NET**

I just returned from a trip to the grocery store and when I got home I sat in my car reviewing my purchases. If you were to pull me over and see my bags, it might appear I was a college student preparing for finals or a pothead planning a road trip.

I had a pint of ice cream, soda (the good kind with real sugar), candy (half eaten already), pasta, burrata, potatoes, cheese, sour cream, blueberries, and small bunch of kale, among other items. Do I have an eating disorder? No. Do I maybe have a problem? Possibly. Am I just like you but you aren't willing to admit it publicly? Even more possibly.

I stress eat. I don't do drugs, I don't drink, and I don't gamble. But I eat…a lot…sometimes! Most of the time I'm pretty good. I don't keep junk food in the house, and my kids are pretty healthy eaters. But I went to the store today and bought what I wanted with no rules. I'm a grown-up! I can buy what I want. And it was marvelous!

I bought Moose Tracks ice cream and got a plastic spoon and ate it in my car. That's right. I'm a rebel. I bought M&M's and real Coke, and I don't even care if it rusts a car. Everything is so controlled right now in my life and not by me, or so it seems. Sometimes I want to be totally, radically in charge of one thing, and I choose food. I can read all the posts about addiction and unhealthy choices I want. But they are not changing these habits. I've been bottoming out for a couple days at a time a few times a year for so long I can't remember. It's usually before a big cleanse or fast, and now it's before a season change in my life and I feel out of control. Maybe it's my way of coping and I'm supposed to feel guilty. But here's the secret: I don't! Eating ice cream all alone is delightful.

Today at the grocery store I was reading a random recipe magazine. I saw this recipe for funeral potatoes. These cheesy goodness potatoes are made for after funerals because they bring people comfort. Yes, Jesus! Carbs, cheese, and potatoes are directly from You. I knew it! The world says carbs are the enemy. But is that really true? ARE they really that bad?

I guess it's like Paul said in 1 Corinthians 6:12: "'Everything is permissible for me,' but not everything is beneficial. 'Everything is permissible for me,' but I will not be mastered by anything" (CSB).

I really thought about this verse, and the last part is what struck me. Paul said, "I will not be mastered by anything." I can joke about my binge eating and funeral recipes, but if I had to give it all up, I could and I would. I'm not mastered by food. I love food. Food is awesome, but it doesn't own me. And if these little adventures at the grocery store are not a monthly or weekly habit, I think I'm okay.

But it's always good to take stock of all our actions and see where we stand. In Matthew 24, God says we cannot serve two masters and I will not bow down to Ben or Jerry! And when I get to heaven I'm quite sure they will not be serving me kale! I bet there were potatoes in the garden of Eden. I just bet!

• • •

## TO THINK ON

- Is there anything in your life you feel mastered by?

- Is there something that is out of balance and out of control?

- What can you do about it?

• • •

*Dear God,*

*You gave me Your Word as good guidelines for life. Allow me to put everything in check as it needs to be. Please don't ever let anything master me that is not good for my soul, mind, or body. And by the way, thank You for creating ice cream!*

*In Jesus' name.*

*Amen.*

# FARM-TO-TABLE FRIENDS

*Two are better than one,*
*because they have a good return for their labor:*
*If either of them falls down,*
*one can help the other up.*
*But pity anyone who falls*
*and has no one to help them up.*

**ECCLESIASTES 4:9-10**

think every woman should have several types of friends in her life.

A prayer warrior friend who will always answer your SOS call.

An old friend who knows all your baggage and loves you anyway.

A farm-to-table friend who cooks, makes crafts, and can help you in life's other SOS moments.

I have all of these women in my life. I just never knew how much I needed number three until my neighbor Bronwyn came into my life. Normally she is the type of woman I would make fun of because she ferments her own sauerkraut and makes the best home-cooked meals and has even talked about buying a chicken for her front yard so she can have fresh eggs. Can you tell she's not from LA? She's from Alaska. She's tall and beautiful in that natural, "I wash my hair with honey and homemade soap" kind of way.

In the past I would let women like Bronwyn intimidate me, because what could I possibly offer her in a friendship? A bag of Cheetos?

But over the years we've struck up a great friendship, and our kids play together. It's awesome how God knew He was going to bring us together before we were ever born.

I decided this time to embrace all the "perfection" that my neighbor represents and use it to my advantage...um, I mean, take an interest in her cooking and canning. We've made Keto desserts and countless jars of sauerkraut and drank homemade kombucha, and I've pretended all along I was helping but really I'd just buy the ingredients and come over and watch her work.

Because she's so crafty, I can't tell you the number of times my kids have run over to her house to borrow glue guns, felt, and wood for whatever diorama or project they were making. One time I ordered Lucy's Maleficent costume for a play and it arrived two sizes too big. The show was the next day, and Bronwyn came over with a needle and thread and saved the day.

I don't have any of her skills, not one, and I've decided not to even pretend I ever will. And honestly, now that we're neighbors, why would I need them? It's good to have a farm-to-table friend who can help my family eat healthy and braid my hair because she watches YouTube tutorials and doesn't have a daughter.

Now, I bet you're wondering, *What is she getting out of this friendship?* I suppose I make her laugh. I let her watch my Academy Award movies DVDs because I get them early since I work in Hollywood. I take her to rooftop films and plan girls' nights at my house without kids. I've seen God at work in this friendship. We take walks together and lament about our sugar habits and talk about life.

She had shared with me that she grew up in differing faith backgrounds and was always very interested in my Christian faith. She was no stranger to church, but her childhood was different from my upbringing. I never wanted to push anything on her, of course. But organically we'd talk about God and prayer, and she even asked about the Bible because she thought it was important to expose her kids to reading it.

Now her family has found a new church and the most wonderful pastors whom I recently met. I don't know how much I had to do with their decision as a family to attend church, but I can tell you I've prayed for them to have a relationship with God that is tangible and real to them. It's exciting to know I might have helped plant a seed.

Recently I got an urgent call that her uncle was in the ICU in Alaska with so many complications they didn't know if he was going to make it through the night. She was in Taiwan and barely made it to the airport. She asked me to pray. She really wanted to seek God. I told her I'd pray and so would my friends. I had people from all over the world praying that very minute. Guess what happened? I'm not kidding when I say he had everything from kidney failure on his last remaining kidney to shingles on his brain. But miraculously, he started to wake up and move his fingers. She made it there to be with him, and everyone in her family was praying. He ended up sitting up, eating, and going home from the hospital. I prayed so hard for her uncle to get better, but I prayed for my friend to know that God loves her and still is doing miracles. She was grateful for the prayers and knows there is no explanation for this miracle except that God did it.

So I'm glad I didn't let my insecurities stand in the way of embracing an incredible friendship. We all bring different things to the table, and I think that's just the way God planned it. Besides, God doesn't want me in the kitchen by myself, and neither does the LA Fire Department.

Sometimes our lives can feel so lonely, and we focus on all that's wrong and what we don't have. Instead, we can look at the wonderful people God has put in our lives—some of them literally next door—if we would just get off our phones to go outside and embrace some real relationships. I will always be grateful for my farm-to-table friend. Because God really does meet all needs. I just had to have the eyes to see it.

• • •

## TO THINK ON

- Do you have a friend who might have seemed intimidating at first but then you realized you are a great pair?
- What do you think you bring to the table in your friendships?

• • •

*Dear God,*

*You know the plans for my life, my friendships, and how You will use me. Thank You for giving me friends I can love and be a witness to without really trying. Thank You for showing up in all our lives and making Yourself real to us, especially when we need to see You loving us.*

*In Jesus' name.*

*Amen.*

Day 37

# ROCKY

*Everyone who competes in the games goes into strict*
*training. They do it to get a crown that will not last, but*
*we do it to get a crown that will last forever. Therefore I*
*do not run like someone running aimlessly; I do not fight*
*like a boxer beating the air. No, I strike a blow to my*
*body and make it my slave so that after I have preached*
*to others, I myself will not be disqualified for the prize.*

**1 CORINTHIANS 9:25-27**

There are certain movies that make me bawl like a baby, but none more than *Rocky*! I've seen every single installment, and I cry every time I watch one of them. The stories are about more than good versus evil. Their focus is more than the knock-out punch. He didn't win in most of the big fights, but he was a champion.

I love the verse in the Bible Paul wrote: "I have fought the good fight, I have finished the race, I have kept the faith" (2 Timothy 4:7). I think Paul would have liked Rocky. Rocky is a true winner in my book.

The reason he is a winner is because he never gave up on his dreams. In real life Sly Stallone wrote this script as a young, unknown actor with $106.00 in his bank account. He showed it to over 100 different producers. No one wanted to take a chance on making the movie, much less having this kid from Philly starring in it. When a studio finally offered to make it, they wanted Burt Reynolds to play Rocky. Stallone could have easily compromised his vision. But instead, he refused the

$360,000 paycheck and waited for the chance to play his dream role. It was a good decision, because that franchise has grossed over $1.4 billion.

If that isn't inspiring, I don't know what is. I mean, if you haven't seen the movie, take a chance and watch it and just tell me you don't feel like running up some stairs with your arms in the air when it's over.

We can seriously learn a lot from this character Rocky. He was humble. He wasn't a showboating boxer when they approached him to fight the champ. Rocky wasn't looking for fame. He just wanted to compete. He wasn't afraid of the challenge, but he knew he needed the right help and to train hard. He also knew the importance of having a good mentor and coach. Mickey pulled no punches and told Rocky he wasn't going to win if he didn't put in the work. He even made Rocky chase a live chicken to improve his speed in the ring. Mickey was also a loving father figure to Rocky and taught him that win or lose, you don't quit. A real champion takes the punches and gets back up. Rocky listened and became a world champion.

In one of the later movies, Rocky was having a talk with his son. He said to him, "You, me, or nobody is gonna hit as hard as life. But it ain't about how hard ya hit. It's about how hard you can get hit and keep moving forward. How much you can take and keep moving forward. That's how winning is done." Rocky had his fair share of hits in and out of the ring. He lost his fortune and even the love of his life, Adrian. But he kept going. Not only that, he paid it forward when he stopped fighting and trained the son of his fiercest opponent, Apollo Creed. He never stopped living his life like a fighter; even when he was battling cancer, he was no quitter.

My eyes are watering just thinking about him. He can teach us so much. No matter what battle we are facing, we have to keep swinging. God created us to be a great fighter. He didn't create us to let the enemy and this fallen world walk all over us. We are champions. We may not win every round, but in the end, we know the final score and who wins the title. There is no denying that. It's what we decide to do in the middle that counts. How are we training? There is no shortcut to being a winner.

As Rocky said, "Every champion was once a contender who refused to give up!" I think God would really like Rocky, and so would some of the great champions of the faith we read about. Those guys in the Bible weren't fictional characters. They fought the good fight just like you and I are. And we will win! We can't give up. There are saints all over heaven rooting for us the way we root for Rocky.

• • •

## TO THINK ON

- Do you relate to Rocky? If so, in what areas of your life do you feel like a contender?

- Do you have a good coach or mentor like Mickey in your life? Would you like one?

• • •

*Dear God,*

*Thank You for giving us the Bible to read about the real life warriors of the faith who fought before us. Thank You for the ultimate champion, Jesus, Your Son, who laid down His life for us to have the ultimate victory. Please encourage me when I need to keep fighting.*

*In Jesus' name.*

*Amen.*

Day 38

# THE GREATEST
# SHOWMAN

*But you, O Lord, are a merciful and loving God,*
*always patient, always kind and faithful.*

**PSALM 86:15 GNT**

was just watching the cooking show *Chopped Junior* with Ruby.
When it was over, she disappeared into the kitchen, saying she was
going to cook for Mommy. I had no idea what to expect, but I was
tired so I didn't interfere. She came back with this truly delicious con-
coction of granola bars, fruit, and nuts all mixed and heated up to perfection. Who knew she could use a microwave? Immediately I emailed
casting, saying I had the next Food Network Star on my hands. I told
her she was going to be a famous chef, and she agreed.

I suppose I'm her biggest cheerleader because that was how I was
raised. My parents assumed I could do anything I wanted and told me
so. When I was interviewing for a private kindergarten, the teacher
asked me what I did in my spare time, and I said I didn't have much
free time because of my job as a Paris fashion hat designer. I told her
how I would design the hats (on my fashion plates stencils #80skids)
and my dad would send them to Paris. I guess I was so convincing she
thought I was a genius and wanted me to skip to first grade.

I was also challenged by my dad to submit for the Guinness Book
of World Records when I was nine years old if I could dribble a basketball 7,000 times without stopping. So we went down in the basement
and I accomplished my goal. I don't think I'm actually in the book,

but my dad claims I'm the champion. I didn't have a childhood without challenges, but my parents helped me overcome all of them and set out for the next goal.

Being raised with that kind of confidence was a key factor in the adult I grew up to be. I set my mind on going to Hollywood to pursue acting, and that's exactly what I did. Though my mom was freaking out I'd end up in church with Tom Cruise. #scientology

My parents didn't tell me all the reasons I wasn't good enough or how hard the odds were going to be. They just told me to work hard, prepare, and follow my dreams. It wasn't easy, but I never thought about failure because that wasn't talked about much in my family. After all, my dad was a marine and my mom was a Vietnam vet. I guess you could say they were high achievers. I'm truly grateful for this kind of upbringing. It allowed me to dream big despite what the world might throw at me.

One of my favorite mom stories is about Pablo Picasso's mom. He said, "My mother said to me, 'If you are a soldier, you will become a general. If you are a monk, you will become the Pope.' Instead, I was a painter, and became Picasso."

We can choose which voices we listen to every day. Do we listen to Dr. Phil and TV experts telling us we have problems or the beauty magazines and Instagram telling us our lives don't measure up?

Do we listen to the naysayers who tell us, "Your dreams will never happen because they are too big"? What about the people in our lives the enemy uses to get us off track of the great plans God has had for our life since before we were born? The devil is not above using humans to hurt us, even at a young age, and make us feel unworthy. If he can accomplish that, he might get us to stop believing in Jeremiah 29:11, where God said, "I know the plans I have for you...plans to prosper you." Think about that. He said "prosper," not settle into something mediocre. God wants to prosper us and the devil wants us to feel victimized. And most of the time the naysayers are being negative because that's all they've ever been taught.

This world isn't an easy place to navigate, and some of you might not have had any human cheerleaders to tell you how amazing you are.

But I must remind you that you have the greatest cheerleader in the entire universe, and He is the one who created it. Just listen to how He feels about you in Isaiah 41:10:

> Do not fear, for I am with you;
> do not be dismayed, for I am your God.
> I will strengthen you and help you;
> I will uphold you with my righteous right hand.

The Bible is filled with passages about how much God thinks you are the greatest thing He ever created. And if the God of all creation is on your side, how can you lose? You are the greatest showman, no matter what you choose to do. So be your own cheerleader today. You're worth it!

• • •

## TO THINK ON

- Can you find some verses about how God thinks you are amazing?
- Take some time to meditate on the verse that's just for you. Pin it to your bathroom mirror and read it every day. Remember, He wrote the book for you!

• • •

*Dear God,*

*When I read Your Word, I want to remember You wrote it with me personally in mind. Your heart breaks when mine does. You cheer for me in every situation. Help me see how much You love me and how much You want things in this life to work out for my good. You gave me these dreams. Let's accomplish them together.*

*In Jesus' name.*

*Amen.*

# AND WE JUST KEEP ROLLING ALONG

*When I am afraid, I put my trust in you.*

**PSALM 56:3**

have never liked roller coasters. I don't know why people pay their hard-earned money to have their stomachs come up through their throats. I do not want to feel that way on purpose.

My daughters approach risk very differently. Lucy was born the daredevil she is today and always has been trying to find ways to fly. Ruby was so cautious we could barely get her on a merry-go-round if the horse was moving up and down. I get it! We don't know these horses or what they are capable of. I've done actual horseback riding up a mountain, and the entire time I was convinced my horse had a death wish and wanted to end it all right there on the cliff. I guess I'm not the biggest risk-taker when it comes to my personal safety.

One Saturday I took my kids to the local carnival. I took one look at some of those rickety, rusty rides and the guys who were running them and I was immediately concerned. One dude took a long smoke break and I was worried he'd forgotten to tighten all the screws to those magic carpet swings. We could go flying at any minute, and it wouldn't be like Aladdin!

Ruby and I decided to hit the rides that were more our speed for the ten-and-under crowd. We started off on the kiddie airplanes and the spinning strawberries that never really spun. Ruby was much braver than she had been before. I was impressed. So then she got her eye on the kiddie roller coaster called "The Orient Express." I thought that seemed like a leisure type of train and I could handle it if she could. I was up for adventure and also looking forward to my caramel apple after we were done.

So after a long, hot wait in the sun, we boarded the ride. The attendant buckled us in, and when I heard that click, I looked up to see I was facing a bit of a bigger hill than I noticed previously. Now, let me put this in perspective. This ride was for ages ten and under, so we're not talking Six Flags Silver Bullet.

I couldn't show fear to my daughter because this was her big leap into riding the "big rides." She looked excited. The ride started with that fateful *click, click, click* up the hill, and there was no turning back. It was slow, and that made it all the more terrifying. Couldn't they just zoom us up and get it over with? Why prolong this feeling of doom? The next thing I knew, my stomach was coming up through my throat and I was being tossed like a salad through twists and turns going a million miles per hour (well, it's all relative!).

Did we get on the wrong ride? Nope, everyone else looked about six or under. I was trying to hold my neck still and wondering how much physical therapy I was going to need. It just kept rolling and rolling. It was the same hill and circle over and over and over. I knew it was going to end in my logical mind, but when? I couldn't mathematically calculate the number of rotations we still had to make. I looked for the emergency release switch but there was none. What idiot wants off the kiddie rides?

And then I looked over at Ruby. She was laughing and even had taken her hands off the bar in sheer delight. She was loving every second. Her face was the expression of abundance and perfect joy. Were we on the same ride? Here I was clinging for my life, trying to avoid whiplash, and this kid was riding fancy-free, waving her hands in the air like she just didn't care. Was this the same kid who wouldn't ride the merry-go-round just a short while ago? Did she know the ramifications of what could happen to us if the ride broke? Of course not! She was having the time of her life.

We were in the *exact* same situation having two completely different experiences. One of us was choosing to trust that the ride operator and the engineers did their job. And the other one was in panic and doubt and letting her thoughts and anxiety ruin her fun. We have choices. Ruby was choosing trust and fun, and I wasn't.

Maybe I had more life experiences of fear to draw from, I rationalized. But had I ever been thrown off a roller coaster before? No. That's why I had the buckle.

That adventure reminds me of how we ride through life. We can choose to trust that God, the engineer and ride operator, knows what He is doing and has an end in mind where we are safe and sound. But He also allows twists and turns along the way because without them life would be boring, like the non-spinning strawberries ride.

It's up to us how we face each experience. Are we going to go through life clutching a bar in fear and terror? Or can we raise our hands in the air, knowing that life can be a roller coaster, and enjoy the ride? I looked at my daughter, laughing her head off, and took my own hands and raised them in the air and screamed with her. It was actually kind of fun, and I knew I earned that caramel apple!

• • •

## TO THINK ON

- How do you approach your life when it feels like a roller coaster? Are your hands in the air in trust or are you clutching the handles in fear?

- What can you do to learn to trust that God has a good outcome when life gets really twisty?

• • •

*Dear God,*

*I know You never promised us life was going to be a smooth, easy ride. Help me have faith that You engineered this roller-coaster ride in the first place. You know the beginning and the end, and I want to enjoy it.*

*In Jesus' name.*

*Amen.*

## TOP TEN THINGS I SHOULD
## LIKE AS AN ADULT BUT DON'T

1. Kale and LaCroix soda water

2. Opera, the ballet, and classical music concerts

3. *Downton Abbey*

4. Hiking (walking up a hill of any kind) or walking anywhere near sand

5. Coffee

6. Natural-flavored ice cream (rosewater, activated charcoal)

7. Financial planning

8. Shakespeare

9. Going to my kids' sporting events

10. Playdates when kids are involved

Day 40

# WOULD GOD FOLLOW YOU?

*If you keep yourself pure, you will be a special utensil for honorable use. Your life will be clean, and you will be ready for the Master to use you for every good work.*

**2 TIMOTHY 2:21 NLT**

Jesus said that if we love Him, we must "take up [our] cross and follow" Him (Matthew 16:24). We're all willing to do that, right? While it's an easy thing to say, can we follow Jesus' example by being so selfless? But I have a question for you. Would Jesus follow you? In today's terms we have taken *follow* to a new meaning, in which one person follows another on a social media platform. I know we say we're willing to let Christ into every part of our lives. But if God were taking a full inventory of every single like, comment, dislike, and post you've ever made...would He choose to follow you? Would He put His name as one of your people who support what you're doing and what you stand for?

We live in a world where it appears that everything is out in the open. But is it? Sometimes people make anonymous comments on Twitter or Yelp reviews that are downright vicious. Sometimes the things we view that come through our feed are less than appropriate but we just assume everyone's watching it, so it's no big deal. Is it really gossip when it's already online? These posts about real people can cause real damage, and by reading them we are a part of the problem.

I am a card-carrying, pro-life advocate Christian, but I tend not to get too political with my social media. It causes havoc most times. But I'm certainly not afraid to support the things I see that are in line with my values. I've been called out on it, but I know anything I respond to is out there on the internet forever, so I try to be respectful. I follow a million pages and ones I believe are making a difference in the world today, such as some of the ministries overseas. I love to see their posts.

I also follow the *Hollywood Reporter* and have spent *way* too many hours obsessing about the #MeToo movement and which Hollywood star is the latest casualty. I've been known to get sucked into reading about a few love triangles involving Kardashians a time or two. I think we all might want to take an inventory of who we are online and offline. Do the actions of both match up? Would you let your friends or even pastors view all your account activity?

We each have our own decisions to make as we post and comment on what we think is Christ honoring. I love commenting on social media, but alas, sometimes people don't love my humor. When I was in New York City I saw this homeless guy with a sign that said, "Why lie! I want beer money!" I thought he was creative and hilarious, so I took my picture with him. I bet even God thought it was funny. I got a nasty email from a lady chewing me out for being "unholy." Now, if she was so proud of what she had to say, why not just post her harsh words online?

What are you like in private messages? Are you always kind? Are you always appropriate? If you are married, have you ever felt you were dangerously close to crossing a line with messaging a member of the opposite sex? I'm guilty of that. I've already told you how I had to cut contact with my ex-boyfriends even though our interactions seemed harmless. I didn't even want the appearance of anything not aboveboard.

Take a look behind the curtain at your behavior online and see if there is anything convicting. God is always there to steer us in the right direction, and He doesn't hold a grudge. Now tune in next time for a full assessment of your Netflix viewing history! Be warned!

* * *

## TO THINK ON

- Do you think God would follow you proudly on social media?
- Is there anything coming to mind you feel a bit convicted about?

• • •

*Dear God,*

*Thank You for giving me the Holy Spirit to guide me on the straight path and direct me back on it when I've veered off a bit. I want everything in my life to be a reflection of my relationship with You.*

*In Jesus' name.*

*Amen.*

# SETTLING...A LITTLE

*Without faith it is impossible to please him, for
whoever would draw near to God must believe that
he exists and that he rewards those who seek him.*

**HEBREWS 11:6 ESV**

dream big, I pray big, and I don't settle for anything. If I pray for someone to be healed, I pray in faith for a miracle. If someone needs encouragement, I'm their biggest cheerleader. When Lucy wanted to be president, I bought her a hat that had "Future President" on it because why shouldn't she go big or go home? She recently decided she wanted to be a Supreme Court justice instead because, in her words, "They can't fire you."

Because of my propensity to challenge myself, it came as a surprise to me when I realized I had become comfortable in some circumstances that were clearly not God's best plans for me. It felt as though the enemy had been at work, but maybe it was only partially the enemy, because I had decided in my heart that this was where God wanted me and it wasn't *so* bad. Have you ever found yourself saying things like, "I could handle this. It's not so awful. At least it's not as bad as _____"?

It's easy to fall into this trap because this world is full of struggles, and sometimes we just want to take a break from all the warfare. There's nothing wrong with that.

But we need to ask ourselves, what are we getting a little too complacent about in our lives? Are we settling just a little? If so, how do we change? I knew I needed to make a move, but I wasn't sure where to begin because I'd been settled with what I had and I was tired. The enemy uses physical and spiritual fatigue to get us off our game and to tempt us to stop pressing into the promises of God. But if we realize that all that negative thinking and lethargy isn't coming from the Lord, we can trace it back to Satan's ever-so-subtle attacks.

Satan doesn't show up with a pitchfork and fire shooting out of his hands. Sometimes Satan shows up as fleeting thoughts in our mind: *I will never do better than this. God can't really use me because...* (fill in the blank). *I'm not as worthy as those other people who did great things for God because* (fill in with excuse number two). These sentiments cannot be coming from God because He is your biggest advocate. Do you know that? He is wild about you, and there are more verses about His love for you than you can even imagine. Just look at Zephaniah 3:17: "He will rejoice over you with gladness; he will quiet you by his love; he will exult over you with loud singing" (ESV).

Can you believe that? Yes, the Maker of heaven and earth is singing about you. Yes, you, reading this right now. Stop and take that in. Now get up and do something about it. God is on your side!

I think fatigue can be a weapon from the enemy's camp to get us to just lie down wherever we are and decide to pitch a tent. But Isaiah 43:2 says, "When you walk through the fire, you will not be burned; the flames will not set you ablaze." God said we are to walk *through* the fire of whatever trials we face, not that we are to stop and get a mani-cure. But when we're battle weary and our faith has been tested time and time again, the enemy might offer us a little respite as a counter-feit for what God really has for us.

Take the Israelites, for example. The Old Testament says it took them 40 years to take a 40-day journey. They murmured and wandered through the wilderness because they didn't have the courage to go in and take the land God had said was theirs. God had made them a promise about going to a wonderful new land. But when they heard there were giants there, suddenly hanging out in the woods with free manna didn't seem so bad. They literally lived in tents and ate the *same* food for 40 years! They were scared of the unknown—and who could blame them?

They were fed and sheltered, but what awaited them was freedom and all the glory they had been promised by God Himself. Maybe the older Israelites were just happy to be out of Egypt and were too tired to fight any more giants after all those years of slavery.

When our past is quite traumatizing, sometimes it's hard to believe the future could be brighter. I'm sure we've all thought, *This is the best I can do*, and then we stop believing God has something better for us. Maybe it's your job that you don't really love, or a relationship that isn't healthy for you, or you're not pursuing your dreams because you don't want to get your hopes dashed again.

I have dreams God has placed in my heart, and I'm not giving up on them. What are your dreams? Maybe you want to go into ministry someday, but it seems too farfetched. What if you are single and you want to get married? Or if you're in a troubled marriage and want God to save it? You don't have to tell what you long for, but most certainly share your dreams with God. He might be the one who gave you those desires in the first place.

God doesn't get glory when we are miserable. We won't win people over to Christ by living that way. And if God's given you something to do for His kingdom, then why not embrace that challenge? He is a big God!

We are no longer slaves, and God wants us walking in freedom and blessing. We just have to believe His Word is true. In fact, He sent His Son to die for our freedom. Now let's go slay some giants!

• • •

## TO THINK ON

- Take a serious look at your life. Is there any area where you feel you've gotten too comfortable, that it's not God's best for you?

- What would it take for you to believe things could change?

• • •

*Dear God,*

*I know You want the best for me. You wrote the Bible for me personally, and I long to believe that You have good plans for my life. Please help me have faith in the areas where I seem stuck. I want to dream again.*

*In Jesus' name.*

*Amen.*

Day 42

# OUT OF THE
# MOUTH OF BABES

*And he said: "Truly I tell you, unless you change and become
like little children, you will never enter the kingdom of heaven."*
**MATTHEW 18:3**

Raising strong-minded, confident, God-fearing children has never been easy. Let's start with the time we were downtown shopping and I lost track of Lucy for one minute. When I found her she was outside the store with dirt on her face. She was holding out her hat and asking for money. I said, "Lucy, what do you think you're doing?" She said, "I'm like Oliver, Mommy. You said yourself that you're not made of money so I decided to help!"

When Lucy was in pre-kindergarten she told me, "Mommy, Henry tried to kiss me today at school." "Did you tell the teacher?" I asked. "Yeah," she answered, "but I let him kiss me first!"

One Mother's Day Lucy said to her dad, "I want to get Mommy something really nice and really valuable!" "That's so sweet, Lucy," her dad responded. Then she said, "Yeah, 'cause when she dies I'm gonna get it!"

When we were at a school parents' night, Ruby looked up at this man, tapped him on the arm, and said, "Are you a boy or a girl?" He looked right at her in total dismay and said in a gruff voice, "I'm a dude!"

One Sunday after church we met the nicest family in the parking lot. The beautiful size 0 mom was holding her toddler, and Ruby pointed to her stomach and said, "You got a baby in there?"

Then there was the time we had just joined a new church. The pastor had asked us kindly to pray for his mother, who was having severe arthritis in her hand. I prayed for her healing, and knowing Lucy loved to pray for healing too, I told Lucy—who was about six at the time—to pray for the pain in her hands. Lucy grabbed this matriarch's hand and said, "Satan, I command you to get the hell off this woman right now!" The pastor's mom, Barbara, looked at me and smiled. "Well, she's right!"

Lucy always loves to pray for people, and the very next week at our new church an elderly woman had a cane and looked sad. We asked if she was in pain and if we could pray for her. Lucy proceeded to pray for her in faith for all her pain to be released, and then she added, "And, God, please take the wrinkles off her face too while You're at it!"

Recently we had a healing prayer night at my church. It was a night where people were scattered all over the church in small groups to pray for healing. I let my kids pray as they felt led, and then I saw Lucy approaching this lady at the altar. I didn't know this group of ladies, but something inside me told me to stay put and let her say whatever she was going to say. I kept praying silently myself with one eye open.

Then I heard a shriek in the direction of my child. The familiar chill went down my spine, and my first thought was, *What did my kid do?* The lady Lucy had been praying for was screaming and crying…in joy. I guess Lucy prayed for her legs and all her pain went away and she was running back and forth, totally healed. I just smiled, and then I saw Lucy going to the next group of ladies with her sister in tow.

A lady in this group had a cane, was in a lot of pain, and could barely stand. Lucy prayed for her as I watched. The elderly lady said she was feeling less pain. She wanted to stand up and try to walk. Just then Lucy grabbed her cane as though she were a 1922 evangelist and said, "See? You won't need this anymore! Get up and walk." I was impressed and dying inside at the same moment. We helped lift the woman up, and she took a few steps. There were tears all around.

The lesson I learned that night was that God gave these children strong wills and bold mouths for a reason. No, it wasn't always to embarrass me in the shopping center, but it was to proclaim the good news of the gospel and set the captives free. I've learned that my job is to shepherd their hearts and continue to instill in them that God is still in the miracle business. He just sometimes enjoys using little girls like them to help pray them into being.

• • •

## TO THINK ON

- Have you ever had someone in your life say something bold but embarrassing?
- How did you handle the situation?
- Do you need a revving up of your faith to be like a child?

• • •

*Dear God,*

*You put children in our lives all around us to remind us of the kind of pure hearts and pure faith that we need. They are unafraid to speak the truth no matter what. Help me return to my childlike faith and to be used by You to help others.*

*In Jesus' name.*

*Amen.*

# THE F WORD

*Say to those with fearful hearts,*
*"Be strong, do not fear;*
*your God will come,*
*he will come with vengeance;*
*with divine retribution*
*he will come to save you."*

**ISAIAH 35:4**

You know the feeling that creeps up your entire body and causes you to be paralyzed for a moment? You feel tingly, you feel uneasy, you feel panicked, and maybe even shaky. You are experiencing a visit from our old friend Fear!

I've read and studied so much on how to handle fear. You'd think I would have mastered it by now. But today just proved I'm not immune to fear...yet.

I don't think fear plagues my everyday life, but it really bothers me when something happens and I immediately have a physical reaction of fear. It's more than picturing the worst-case scenario. My body tenses up with stress and fear of what might happen and I feel frozen like Lot's wife!

I had to visit the doctor awhile back, and she prescribed an antibiotic because she thought I had an infection. I have a 30-year history of taking antibiotics, but about 10 percent of the time I've had severe, even life-threatening reactions to certain drugs. I've ended up in the hospital unable to breathe or broken out in hives. So you could say I have good reason to literally and physically freak out. After I took that little pill, I felt tingly and my nerves were on edge as I was looking for even the tiniest sign of an allergic reaction to pop up. I was doing my best not to obsess over the situation, so I went in my room and put on some music, one of my favorite songs: "No Longer Slaves."

The song lyrics went right to my heart. They talk about the Lord parting the Red Sea so we could walk right through it. The song shouts praise to the God who delivers us.

I needed to have those words permeate my mind and my soul. I needed a tangible reminder that God is for me, not against me. While I listened I had to fight all the thoughts of the past and the bad things that have happened to me, despite my prayers. I had to remember I'm *still* here! I've come through every single one of those trials. And like the song says, God parted the Red Sea for me. That is huge! He loves me that much, and He loves you that much too!

So call me dramatic, but taking that medication felt as though I was standing at my own personal Red Sea moment. I didn't want to end up in an ambulance again, barely breathing with my throat closing up like I had several times before. But I choose not to turn back in fear but to jump into the sea with a cleared path ahead of me.

We have to take control over the thoughts that turn into emotions that can paralyze us in our tracks. Fear cannot stop you today, and God willing, fear will not stop you tomorrow.

God gives me reminders time and time again that I am not alone. God is always watching over me. God wants to help me overcome these feelings of fear. If we can hammer that point home, I think we can find the victory. Fear is not from God. Therefore, fear does *not* have a place in our lives. We have the ability to take control and tell it to leave. We can find peace right now with God.

I made up this acronym:

**F**—Forget what you know from the past and look to the present, knowing God has you in the palm of His hand.

**E**—Everyone is going to have opinions. Only take in what seems to line up with God's Word (stay off WebMD).

**A**—If you feel fear coming at you, take authority over it and speak the Word of God and tell it to leave.

**R**—Read God's promises of delivering you from fear over and over until they stick in your head.

You do not have to be a slave to fear. You are a freed child of God. Jesus paid the price for your freedom. You just have to accept it as paid in full! If we don't do that we are disrespecting what He died for. He wants to give us all the freedom He has already paid for. Remember what God wrote about the Proverbs 31 Woman: "She can laugh at days to come" (verse 25). She was free of fear, and you can be too. Today is your day! Leave your fear behind and let freedom ring!

• • •

## TO THINK ON

- How much has fear caused you pain and heartache in your life?
- If you could do it over, would you use your authority to tell fear to leave?

• • •

*Dear God,*

*Thank You for giving me the authority to cast fear out of my mind. I can speak to that spirit and simply say, "Fear, I command you to leave me right now in the name of Jesus." And it must flee. Your words are powerful and true. Help me use them when they are needed.*

*In Jesus' name.*

*Amen.*

# GOD SPEAKS AT TARGET

*God is able to bless you abundantly, so that
in all things at all times, having all that you
need, you will abound in every good work.*

**2 CORINTHIANS 9:8**

have many talented friends, and Suzie is one of my favorites. She makes me laugh while encouraging me to be a better person. Below is Suzie's story about God meeting our every need.

• • •

Off I went to Target very pregnant and having some rather painful and consistent contractions, but I was desperately in need of groceries. I was also desperately in need of an outfit that would do a better job of hiding my swollen everything—other than my recent uniform of leggings. So off I went with my contractions, my toddler, and a very tight budget. Babies are expensive, plus we had just bought our first house and I was feeling very fearful about finances.

After two hours of waddling through the store carefully choosing my groceries, price comparing everything, putting back items I convinced myself we didn't need, then throwing them back into the cart once I remembered that my husband and daughter did need to eat something other than toast and sauceless spaghetti, I selected the cheapest outfit I could find—one that I hoped would make me feel feminine, attractive, and a little less like Shrek.

We arrived at the checkout counter, where I watched carefully as the bill rose far past my tight budget, and then I panicked. I blurted out, loudly enough for the whole store to hear, "I'm not going to need that," referring to the outfit I had had such high hopes for. I paid the bill and walked out of the store, livid at myself for buying so many groceries. *How did I let this happen! There are only three of us in our family!* I hastily loaded the groceries into the trunk fatigued, contracting, and swollen. Then I felt a rush of fear hit me.

I quickly pulled out of my parking spot still reeling from the cost of my groceries and just as I did—*ding*—a text came from a friend. She was out of food and her rent was late. After reading her text I continued driving toward home, though I don't know why. Truthfully, as soon as I read her text I knew I was not going home at all. I pulled over to the side of the road and asked her to text me her address.

Suddenly, the Holy Spirit spoke. "Why are you so afraid?" Instantly I was taken back to a time when I myself was living in a very similar situation as my friend, unsure of where my next meal or paycheck would come from, unsure of where God was. The Holy Spirit had spoken to me all those years ago and said, "Give Me time to provide," and He had and continued to do so. In fact, He had provided more than I could have fathomed, far beyond money, groceries, and rent. Indeed, why was I so afraid? I took deep breath and my spirit calmed at the reminder of His faithfulness.

Minutes later I met my friend outside of her home where we divided the groceries, both of us aware that this abundance hadn't come from me at all but from our heavenly Father. No longer angry at myself for buying too much, now the items I agonized over buying were the tangible signs His provisions were for not just my family but also for my friend. God was aware of her need long before I received her text. Just as He was aware of mine.

See, my friend needed groceries, and I needed to be reminded that I do not need to fear. When we give, even with trembling hands, what He has given to us, it is more than an act of obedience but one of faith, trust, and worship. When we tune our hearts to His promptings, God is waiting to meet the needs of our bodies and our souls.

• • •

## TO THINK ON

- Have you ever had an experience where God blessed you to be a blessing?
- Is giving something that comes easily to you or is it a struggle?
- How could you ask God to help you overcome any obstacles being able to give more freely and not live in fear?

• • •

*Dear God,*

*Help me remember You provide for my every need. Even when I am in fear, help me take a moment to realize You know what lies ahead and what blessings You have in store for me.*

*In Jesus' name.*

*Amen.*

# MAMA HAD A ROLLING STONE

*They cried out to the LORD in their trouble,*
*and he delivered them from their distress.*

**PSALM 107:27**

I've been blessed to have firsthand knowledge that Satan is real and that would be in the form of my many illustrious bouts with kidney stones. If you haven't had one, just picture the pain of childbirth with no baby at the end.

Ironically, you cannot predict when these dreaded attacks will strike. You are just all of a sudden doubled over in horrific pain, as I was a few months ago. I got a call that I had gotten this writing dream job I have been waiting for, and within minutes I had this excruciating pain flood through my lower back. It was all too familiar. I didn't want it to be a kidney stone, and I prayed so hard that it wasn't. I tried to walk around and I prayed and asked for wisdom. I finally opened my Bible, and what literally popped out at me was the verse, "I have set my face like flint" (Isaiah 50:7). When I looked up the word *flint*, I found it means "hard stone." God speaks clearly sometimes. I was suffering from a kidney stone.

I went to the ER as the pain increased to epic proportions. I was dreading the long wait and thought of bringing cash with me to bribe the registration clerks. I was signing in when I looked up and saw Terri, a friend of mine from church who also leads the prayer team. She was like an angel, and I don't know who she bribed, but she got me in a room in three minutes. She laid hands on me and prayed, and my pain levels went down. I felt better, but I had so much fear gripping me from past experiences with stones. I've had surgeries before, and I didn't want to relive that experience. I kept repeating, "I trust You, Lord, to deliver me from evil."

I didn't know how this was going to end up, but God had ordained the circumstances to help me so far. After an ultrasound showed a kidney stone, I ended up chatting with Terri about God's faithfulness as I received IV fluids. Terri even drove me home that night, and we sat in her car praying and talking about how we'd like to birth a young women's ministry in our church.

I was grateful for Terri that night and came home and was able to sleep in peace…that is, until 5:00 a.m. the next morning, when I was in agony and headed back to the hospital for a CT scan. I had to battle my thoughts of anxiety and expecting the worst-case scenario. Surgery not only is horrific but takes you out of commission for weeks, and I couldn't afford that with my work/mom/life schedule and the fact I just got this big new writing job.

While I was in the ER, I texted my sweet friend in Texas who relayed the news she had lost her mother that very day. I continued to pray for them in the midst of my own pain. My kidneys felt like they were on fire, and I made it through the X-ray, hoping the doctors could find some way to help me avoid surgery. I hobbled to the ladies' room barely able to stand. I will spare you the details, but let me just say that right there in that restroom, the stone passed! I was so overjoyed I ran to the hospital gift shop and bought myself an ice cream cone.

I've spent the last couple days recovering from what feels like being run over by a truck. But I just keep saying in my head: "Lord, You delivered me from evil!" The enemy meant for that stone to ruin me, ruin my ministry and schedule, but most of all ruin me with fear. It wasn't easy. I'm not glad it happened, and God certainly didn't cause it to teach me any lessons. But that doesn't mean we can't learn from these crazy situations.

In all circumstances we have to trust God. It even helps if you say that you trust Him out loud. The devil hates that. He wants you to curse God, not trust Him. But just like all those who walked before us in the Bible, we can put our trust in God to see us through anything and He will never let us down. Even when the circumstances are extremely painful and don't turn out the way we wished, we can still trust God. We can still know that He will, *no matter what*, see us through.

. . .

## TO THINK ON

- What is the hardest thing you've gone through lately?
- Were you battling fear?
- Was it hard to trust God?

. . .

*Dear God,*

*In Your Word You say, "When you pass through the rivers, they will not sweep over you" (Isaiah 43:2). Thank You for clarifying I will not stay in that stormy sea. You will always find a way to dry land. Thank You for seeing me through the many storms in this life.*

*In Jesus' name.*

*Amen.*

# PAIN HURTS!

*My God, My God, why have you forsaken me?*
*Why are you so far from saving me, from the words of my*
*groaning? O my God, I cry by day, but you do not answer,*
*and by night, but I find no rest. Yet you are holy,*

**PSALM 22:1-3 ESV**

guess you could say if there was a health lottery, my family and I didn't win. I had several life-threatening health issues and a major spinal reconstruction surgery by the time I was 11. I've survived many more surgeries, near-death medical drug reactions, and too many kidney stones for me to count. Will I get some kind of medal for this in heaven? Will my crown be filled with kidney stones? Because if it is, it would be *very* rocky and not attractive. My mom and dad have been through the ringer with health ordeals themselves, with three bouts with breast cancer and incurable disorders, and my sweet brother becoming an epileptic at age 33. But somehow we are still standing. I don't know how, but by the grace of God we are not dead.

You might find a lot of this ironic, because for the past 13 years I've been passionate about healing prayer and ministry, and I've seen miracles that would blow your mind. I've seen instant healing happen right before my eyes. But I've never seen that kind of miracle happen in my life. I've prayed till I was blue in the face when I've been faced with surgeries for God to heal me, and even then I've gone through procedures with terrible recoveries.

There are many theories out there about how to pray, when to pray, and what to say to God in these trying situations. Everyone has an opinion. And I know the enemy is the author of all of that legalism that makes us feel bad when things don't turn out like we wanted. He is whispering how we didn't pray right or we wouldn't have had to suffer. And that's just not true. That's not in the Bible, and I refuse to believe it.

I know there is power in the tongue and my words matter. I know that prayer makes a difference. But I also know God is not a stranger to pain. He is not immune to suffering because He Himself, in human form, cried out the night before He was going to be crucified, "Father, if you are willing, take this cup from me" (Luke 22:42). He didn't want to hurt if there was a way to avoid it.

When people tell me I just have to speak positive words 100 percent of the time, I ask them if they've ever read the Psalms. What do you think David was doing when he was crying out to God? I think about David when he was living in a cave, trying to save his own life. He not only complained, he cried out in anguish, and God still called him a man after His own heart. I'm sick of well-meaning people telling me I can't share my hurt with God. That somehow He can't handle my frustrations and even anger. He's God! He even warned me I'd face trouble, but He said, "Take heart! I have overcome the world" (John 16:33). I think God wants to hear from us in all situations, when we're happy and thankful and when we're full of grief and pain. Who else is better equipped to handle it than Him?

God can take our honest prayers. We can approach His throne and say, "Father God, I know You love me. I know You gave Your Son to die for me and He said He died for my sins and for all my infirmities. Why do I have to hurt so much? I just want it to end, and I have to believe You do too. Help me not to quit and get bitter, but right now I really need You to move on my behalf. Would You please do that and send Jesus and His angels and whoever else You need to down to earth to help me this instant? I have to keep believing You will deliver me from this evil. I'm doing my best to praise You through this storm. It's just really, really hard right now and I'm sure You understand. I love You always."

I don't know what the specific outcome is going to be of my present health obstacle. But I am a living testimony that He's gotten me through every single challenge I've faced before this. I'm still standing, and that makes His record perfect. So whatever you might be facing today, remember that there is no shame in telling God how you really feel. He can handle it, and not only that, He loves when you are honest with Him.

• • •

## TO THINK ON

- When you are hurting or upset, do you feel comfortable going to God?
- Where else do you turn to for comfort before taking your situations to the Lord?

• • •

*Dear Lord,*

*Thank You for giving me the example of David and those who walked before me and faced many trials. They trusted You with all their emotions, even when they weren't polite and pretty. Thank You for being a big enough God to hear the cry of my heart through broken tears. I won't withhold my feelings from You.*

*In Jesus' name.*

*Amen.*

# JESUS SCHOOL

*Faith comes from hearing, and hearing*
*through the word of Christ.*
**ROMANS 10:17 ESV**

When I was a child I was enrolled in every Bible school west of the Mississippi. It was free daycare! I'm a mom now, so I get it. Horse camp was expensive; Bible school was free, and they provided the snacks!

I'm a church-going adult who works in ministry and hosts prayer meetings. But not too long ago I fulfilled a longtime dream of mine. I went to what I would call "Jesus school" for four days in Dallas. I love conferences, and I used to attend many more than I have recently. I long for the time my friends and I would jump in the car to road trip to hear our favorite evangelist, just to experience a touch from God. We'd spend hours in worship and prayer rooms for several days, and it was always refreshing to my spirit.

I've been a longtime fan of some old-school pastors who helped me through some tough times. These are the guys I'd be watching at 2:00 a.m. while I had a baby struggling to survive in the NICU, and their sermons gave me the encouragement from the Word of God to fight for my daughter's healing.

The messages are simple, to the point, and sometimes incredibly funny. So some of my all-time favorite pastors have this big convention in Dallas every summer, and it's free to attend. About 10,000 people show up, and there's a free kids' camp that teaches the Bible. I've always wanted to go but could never make it work. I travel so much as it is that it felt frivolous to take off to Dallas without a gig. But I needed something to give me a good kick in the pants of faith. And conferences are amazing when you are in an environment of such faith with so many other believers from all over the world. So I asked Lucy if she wanted to join me and got our tickets. I didn't know a soul there. But I went with the expectation I would hear from God.

When we arrived I got a text from a friend in the area. She was willing to come hang out with me at the convention. What an unexpected treat. Jen met me in the morning, and we got Lucy checked in. She had no idea what to expect and was quite the trooper going in alone.

There were sessions all day and night, and I didn't know what kind of attention span I would have, but I was game to give it my best shot. A year ago I was in this very same huge convention center performing on the main stage for 13,000 people. Now I sat alone in the balcony with my Bible and my notebook, hanging on to the pastor's words and trying to take it all in. I learned new things. I was reminded of old truths. And the biggest lesson I took from that week was that God never changes. He is and always was good. He didn't move; we just live in a fallen world.

But I had become a bit battle weary in "doing good." I really needed for God to get me alone in a crowd of 10,000 and get me away from my daily grind so I could focus on Him. It was like getting an IV of good spiritual vitamins from the worship, teaching, and prayers.

I never got called out to publicly pray. I didn't perform or sit with the speakers in the front. But I didn't need any of that. I needed the simple truths, and they refreshed my soul. And when it was over, I had to make a choice to take all that refreshment with me.

I wonder if the Proverbs 31 Woman got to attend events like this? Can you imagine who was preaching? Um…can we say some of the greatest of all time? Did she ever go see Samson do weight-lifting exhibitions? I wonder what kind of crowd she ran with at the watering hole.

If you haven't experienced anything like this conference or spiritual retreat, I highly recommend going to one. Even if you can't get away physically, listen to a series of podcasts or sermons to get you fired up. I recommend keeping a journal while you listen and jotting down verses that are quoted or wisdom that you can apply to your own life.

This experience also made me appreciate having a church to attend on a weekly basis. Being in a room with God's people and worshiping Him together is really special. I know there are a million excuses the devil will throw at us about not getting up and going to church on Sundays. But I think we all know God created the church as a body and a building for a reason, and that is to revive and refresh us as one family. Think about all the time we commit to our physical health. But what are we doing for our spiritual health on a regular basis?

When the conference was over, Lucy said, "Mom, can we come for the whole week next year?" I said, "Probably so, honey! This is cheaper than horse camp! And they have snacks!"

• • •

## TO THINK ON

- What are you doing for your spiritual health?
- Have you considered attending a conference or retreat where you could spend some alone time with God? Why or why not?

• • •

*Dear God,*

*Thank You for allowing me the opportunity to fellowship with You, when I can be away from all that tugs me in the world. Please allow for more times in my life where I can focus on Your beautiful truths and revive my spirit.*

*In Jesus' name.*

*Amen.*

# IT TAKES A MOUSE

*If you are faithful in little things, you will be faithful*
*in large ones. But if you are dishonest in little things,*
*you won't be honest with greater responsibilities.*

**LUKE 16:10 NLT**

'll never forget the day Lucy came home and lamented with great despair that she got cast as "The Farmer" in *The Sound of Music*. She had her heart set on Maria, even though she was five at the time. We explained to her there were no small parts, just small little actors they had to make parts for because parents paid for theater camp. Okay, in reality her dad and I excitedly exclaimed, "Isn't it the farmer who tells the Von Trapps to go in the mountains to escape Austria? Without the farmer there is no show! You save the day! (Even though you have no lines.) You will point in the direction of the mountains and the Von Trapps will go off to freedom because of you (and because the director added this lovely character at the last minute)!"

I had the same experience in my school play as a kindergartner in *The Lion, the Witch and the Wardrobe*. I was cast as one of the mice. You know, the mice that chew off the strings that were binding Aslan the Lion? Yes, I was a freedom fighter as well, with no lines. But I crushed that role of "Mouse" and I was promoted to "Caterpillar #7" in *Alice in Wonderland* later with…one line!

In thinking back on humble beginnings, I'm reminded that what is true in theater is true in life. Every part matters. You can't have a play without a complete cast and crew. You need people to say the lines, hang the lights, stage manage, and yes, clean up the theater. You need people to play big roaring lions and tiny mice. There is no production without every member doing their job. Jesus said it was that way for us too. He compared us to the human body. Every part matters to make the body work properly.

> So the body is not made up of just one part. It has many parts. Suppose the foot says, "I am not a hand. So I don't belong to the body." By saying this, it cannot stop being part of the body. And suppose the ear says, "I am not an eye. So I don't belong to the body." By saying this, it cannot stop being part of the body. If the whole body were an eye, how could it hear? If the whole body were an ear, how could it smell? God has placed each part in the body just as he wanted it to be. If all the parts were the same, how could there be a body? (1 Corinthians 12:14-19 NIrV).

I spent many formative years in theater. Being a part of a theater production gave me the first sense of belonging I can remember. We were all part of making something special together.

I'm blessed that I've had the chance to give my kids that same gift. Ruby rocked the "Spoon" in *Beauty and the Beast* last summer and launched into her own unprompted kickline on stage all by herself! (Improv, baby! She's a star!)

When I went on to work in TV and film productions, I saw the value of a great team. The crew on the *Tonight Show* under the leadership of Jay Leno stayed together for 30 years. I was blessed to be on the show about 25 times. The way Jay greeted each and every person and shook their hand set the tone on his set that each person was important. Even when I had a tiny part in a sketch, they gave me a dressing room with my name on it and a star on it. I learned a lot from leaders like Jay, and some of my fondest Hollywood memories are working on that show. If you make each person on your team feel worthy and valued, they will be loyal to you and give you their very best effort.

I started my career as a tiny mouse chewing some rope and freeing a lion, and now I make my living sharing the gospel, and in some cases, setting the captives free. I pray for salvation, I pray for healing, and I get to do it from the stage.

At the end of the Narnia Chronicles, when the heroes finally reach the end of the world, Reepicheep (leader of the mice) implores Aslan to let him enter his country (or heaven). Aslan allows him to enter, knowing he had his freedom because of the bravery of those mice risking their lives for him. The Word of God says:

> His master replied, "Well done, good and faithful servant! You have been faithful with a few things; I will put you in charge of many things. Come and share your master's happiness!" (Matthew 25:23).

God has much for us to do while on this earth, and we need each other for the greater good of furthering His kingdom. So the next time you feel like a lowly mouse in a lion's world, remember, without the mice Aslan would not have gained his freedom!

• • •

## TO THINK ON

- What situations in your life do you sometimes feel like a bit part instead of a leading player?
- What is the truth about those situations? How is God using you right where you are?

• • •

*Dear God,*

*Please help me have a great understanding of how all parts work together for good. In the times when I feel like a lowly mouse, please remind me of my worth that is in You.*

*In Jesus' name.*

*Amen.*

# WORDS, WORDS, WORDS

*Death and life are in the power of the tongue:*
*and they that love it shall eat the fruit thereof.*

**PROVERBS 18:21 KJV**

think I learned early on the principal of "the power of the tongue." In the classic book *The Little Engine That Could*, that little blue train made it up the mountain with sheer willpower, repeating, "I think I can! I think I can!" He saved the day, and everyone lived happily ever after. His words had the power to help him persevere up those steep tracks!

I've known words have power from the time I was in kindergarten and told Brandon Davis on the playground I loved him. He abruptly ran away. My words were just too "powerful" for him.

Another memory is of my third-grade teacher, Mrs. Veenstra, calling me to her desk and saying, "Kerri, I'm very disappointed in you. I never thought I'd see this behavior from you." I idolized Mrs. Veenstra, and hearing those words from her cut me like a knife. Some kids had been picking on a girl in my class, and I guess I didn't do much to stop it. I might have even joined in; it's a blur. But I do know I could have used my words to help save a fellow classmate from pain and heartache, but I chose not to. How many times have you stood by when gossip was happening or someone was being hurt and said nothing? If we do nothing to stop it, we are part of the problem.

Mrs. Veenstra shared in a simple way that she thought highly of me and that she expected me to be kind and loving to all my fellow students, no matter what. I was mortified and cried myself to sleep.

But let me tell you, as God is my witness, I never made fun of anyone on or off the playground like that again! (Well, except my family, but I get paid for that.) I was never a mean girl. Mrs. Veenstra used her words to change me, and I never forgot it and I am eternally grateful. Yes, our words have power. And a lot of those lessons were not learned in a Bible class, but out there living life, reading books, and being an elementary school kid. And they stayed with me to this day.

It's not too late to learn this simple truth: our words mean something and have an impact, whether it's good, bad, or ugly. Let's try to focus on the good. The world does a good job of speaking ugly!

When is the last time you wrote someone an encouraging note or email for no reason? It could change someone's entire day to hear something positive about themselves. Get crazy, use a pen! Get even crazier and use your voice. Call someone on the phone and tell them you've been thinking about them. Blow their mind that you still know how to dial. People need to hear good things about themselves from a real, live human being. Social media has warped our sense of validation. A spoken word from a friend or coworker could be life-changing.

Life is short, and we shouldn't put off until tomorrow what can be said today. In the words of the other great philosopher, Jerry McGuire, "We live in a cynical world." So don't ever take for granted the power of your words to uplift, encourage, and inspire yourself and those around you. And like my mama always said: "If you can't say something nice… come sit by me!" Oh, wait, was that what she said? See? Words matter!

· · ·

## TO THINK ON

- Think about your life lately. How have words affected you, good or bad?

- Who is there in your life you could speak to who would need it right now?

· · ·

*Dear Lord,*

*Thank You for being the master of words and creating this marvelous thing we call language. Please help me know how to use it appropriately, for good, not evil.*

*In Jesus' name.*

*Amen.*

# POPULAR

*For we are His workmanship, created in Christ*
*Jesus for good works, which God prepared*
*beforehand that we should walk in them.*

**EPHESIANS 2:10 NKJV**

met a popular girl at church; her name was Betty. She was 87. I hung out with Betty, Verian, and the other cool chicks who went through the weekly prayer requests. When I was new at the church and didn't know where I fit in, I saw that was where all the action was. And I thought if I hung out with the holy girls, all of whom were over 80, people would think I was holy too. I walked up to Betty one day and said, "Hi! My name is Kerri. I heard you bake. I eat! So can we hang out at your house?" That's how we became friends.

Betty was a very Proverbs 31 Woman. She had the cutest house on the block, she did her own gardening, and she made her own jam from the fruit trees in her yard. She loved crafts and serving at church. She lived alone and was a delight to everyone she met. One time Betty and I signed up to go on a mission trip to Mississippi. She called it "fellow shopping!" She told me she wasn't opposed to getting married again, so now I had competition for the single fellas!

Betty took her first ever plane trip with me when we went with some church folks to help build houses in Mississippi. Since I am allergic to manual labor, they put me with Betty on the kitchen committee so we could work where it was air-conditioned. One day we were sitting on the bunkbeds in our bedroom, and Betty said something like, "Everyone thinks I'm so perfect."

I said, "Um, yeah, why do think I'm hanging out with you?"

She laughed and said, "I'm not perfect; it's just that everyone who has dirt on me has already died!"

I replied, "Oh really? How did that happen, Betty?"

We both giggled. She had a wonderful sense of humor. And then she started to tell me about her past, her struggles in her life and marriage, and even mistakes she wasn't proud of. I had never heard "church ladies" talk about sinning. I had assumed once you join a church you needed to be done with all that stuff or they would find out and kick you out.

When Betty took off her "perfect church" mask, her vulnerability did something to me. It was like she was giving me a gift to see her imperfections and even her insecurities. She was 87, and she still had insecurities. This floored me. I wondered why more people in church weren't talking about their flaws because it would have helped me feel as though I wasn't alone.

Betty and a lot of my new friends at church had a true desire to continue growing and changing and seeking God. The more they chased after God, the more He could speak into their lives. They were giving Him permission to get involved, even if it looked messy—and some of their stories were quite big disasters before God stepped in.

What I learned from Betty on that trip, and from others afterward, is this: God isn't afraid of our messes. God isn't this angry father figure keeping a scorepad of all our wrongs. He's never said to anyone, "You, My friend, are way too big of a screwup. I could never use you!" He can and will use anyone, if we are willing to be used.

I wanted to be used by God in my life, but I was always worried I wasn't good enough. So I went on mission trips and served on committees with some weird idea that I would earn enough points to get into heaven. I'd been in church all my life, but I had never truly accepted the assurance of my salvation.

Have you ever felt that way? Have you ever felt that you needed to do more to earn God's approval and love? It's hard not to relate God to earthly parents and authority figures. It's hard to imagine there is an all-knowing, loving Father who created the entire universe, and He wants to love on our imperfect, hot-mess selves.

I also know there is a devil out there, and he makes it his job to convince us we will never overcome these struggles. He wants us to believe we are definitely disqualified from being of any service to God's kingdom, so we might as well accept that fact and stop trying to better ourselves. He tries to convince us not to even bother to draw closer to a God who could never love us, much less use us, because we'll never be good enough as long as we keep messing up. Every time we do something wrong, the devil is ever so quick to be right there in our ear, saying, "You did it again! See? I told you. You're never going to change, so just relax and live your life."

There is another voice there too, but sometimes it's much harder to hear over all the clamoring, confusion, and guilt. There is the voice of God saying, "Hey, kid, get back up. I see you have a few scrapes and bruises, but this is a marathon, not a sprint. Let Me help clean you up, and let's see how we can learn from this and do better next time." God doesn't cause us to do stupid things, and honestly, neither does the devil. We have to be willing to own our choices, good and bad. As we grow in our walk with God, we become more mature and more self-aware, and that is a very good thing.

That time in my life with Betty was very special, and we stayed friends until she went to heaven at the ripe young age of 100, still active on her prayer list and cooking until the day she died!

• • •

## TO THINK ON

- Have you ever had a "Betty "in your life? If so, what did you learn from her?

- Do you ever feel like you don't measure up enough to serve God?

• • •

*Dear God,*

*Thank You for sending Your Son to wash away all my sins. I know that because I am a believer in You I qualify to serve You. Please show me the opportunities You want me to say yes to in helping Your kingdom grow. I love You.*

*In Jesus' name.*

*Amen.*

# WORKING (IT) OUT

## With My Friend, Claire Lee

*The LORD is near to all who call on Him,*
*To all who call on Him in truth.*

**PSALM 145:18 NKJV**

eople in LA are mean and say things like, "Do you want some kale?" One time I was feeling rather melancholy and my friend, we'll call her Claire, because that's her real name, said to me, "Kerri, just meet me at the gym. We'll work this out on the treadmill."

I said, "Claire, that is so LA!" I need some good Midwest friends to come over to my house with a cheesy casserole and a Ryan Gosling movie and help me eat my emotions, not drag me to the gym. I strongly feel that the Proverbs 31 Woman would have made me a scarf of fine linen and serious matzoh ball soup and come to my house to comfort me with new clothes and carbs, which I am certain is God's love language! I know some of you actually enjoy this thing called exercise, so I thought I'd let Claire talk about it. I must add that Claire has extremely gorgeous legs and eats a lot of carrots, while I choose chocolate. The following excerpt was written by Claire. I suppose we should give her a chance to defend herself.

• • •

I feel as though I'm constantly running, literally, from one thing to the next. Drop the kids at school, do school stuff, do church stuff, do work stuff, run errands, pick up kids, try to do more work, do homework, make dinner, all at one time. Talk about multitasking! I can never quite catch up, and when I almost do, it all gets away from me again. I write lists, long ones, of everything I need to get done. From simple things like "fold the laundry" and "pick up so-and-so's kid" to "do taxes" and "get that script done." But no matter what, there's always something on the list that doesn't get done (sometimes it's dinner, but that's why I have boxes of mac 'n' cheese).

However, what almost always gets done is exercise. I know it sounds superficial and wrong that I might forgo shopping for groceries to work out, but it's what keeps me from losing my mind. Why? Because exercise allows me to lose my mind—in a good way, of course, in a way where you just let your thoughts go. It's the one time in the day where there's actually quiet in my life. There are no kids begging me for things, no adults asking me questions, and no one wondering when I'll be done with a project.

Some people might hear God in a church service, in prayer, or during worship, but I hear God when I'm exercising. Maybe it's because the pain of the physical act of doing it can be so intolerable that I'm forced to talk to God, or maybe it's because I actually stop doing everything else and just listen. I put on worship music and go. I will listen to a slow-moving, powerful song about Jesus dying for our sins and push through another set of lunges.

If I'm really feeling ambitious, I'll go outside for a run. I only do that when I'm really desperate. I run over to this hike they call "the Stairs" and make my way up the mountain before running back home. That workout is especially difficult, and I find myself having long conversations with God.

You see, I can't control my life. And that's okay. I can, however, control the number of chest presses I do or how many miles I run. I've also learned that nothing goes as planned and something always comes up, but when I make sure to carve out that half hour or an hour to exercise, everything looks brighter. I also feel better, and it forces me to take a shower earlier in the day, which I'm sure other people appreciate.

The great thing about working out is it doesn't just build physical endurance, it also builds life endurance. As it says in James 1:2-3, "Consider it all joy, my brethren, when you encounter various trials, knowing that the testing of your faith produces endurance" (NASB). If I can push through the physical pain of exercise, I know I can push through the challenges of life that come my way daily. And by making time to exercise, I get that special time with God and He helps me work (it) out.

• • •

## TO THINK ON

- Do you have something in your life that is really important not to skip, like working out?
- How does it help you? Does it help you spiritually?

• • •

*Dear Lord,*

*Thank You for creating our bodies to do amazing things and hear You in all different ways. Thank You for speaking to me in just the perfect place and specific way You know I need to hear You.*

*In Jesus' name.*

*Amen.*

# GOOD IDEA VS. GOD IDEA

*If any of you lacks wisdom, you should ask
God, who gives generously to all without
finding fault, and it will be given to you.*

**JAMES 1:5**

wish I had learned the lesson very early on that every harebrained scheme I've come up with in my life wasn't exactly divine intervention. Sometimes the results ended up looking more like a bad sitcom than the way I pictured the scene in my brain. For instance, when I was in eighth grade my parents put me in a new school. All the kids were coloring their hair with this cool stuff called Pizzazz, and it made your hair awesome colors like pink and gold.

Well, my friend Jennifer and I wanted to try it and help me make my big debut. So she slathered all this goop in my hair and I went to sleep. I woke up to her expression of utter horror. I didn't look like Molly Ringwald but more like a hot-pink Troll doll—the one no one bought. It was horrible, and then we looked at the spray can and realized we'd accidentally bought ZAZOO permanent hair color! My mother threatened my life, and I promised her I would fix it. That's when I had my next great idea.

I went in my grandpa's medicine cabinet and grabbed some peroxide and poured it on my head thinking it would make me look like Marilyn Monroe. But it came out tie-dye and I looked like Marilyn Manson! I thought God had led me to that peroxide bottle to help me save the day. But who are we kidding? God doesn't use peroxide. He's more of a Pizzazz guy.

This same lesson goes for the time I bought self-tanner at Dollar Tree and put it all over my dad's bald head before our beach vacation. Don't even ask how that turned out. If he wasn't bald to start with, he would have ended up that way. Or there was the time when I was five and I wanted a bubble bath so I looked under the sink and put Scrubbing Bubbles in the tub. Oh…yes…Scrubbing Bubbles bleach cleaner. By the grace of God, I was saved by my mother before all my skin was burned off.

A few months ago almost-11-year-old Lucy had this big idea for her birthday. She wanted to start a Christian YouTube Channel and help people learn about Jesus. My daughter has always been called to evangelism because she has her father's kind heart and her mother's big mouth. She was so excited her eyes were glistening with possibilities. She was literally researching "Child Evangelists" until the wee hours of the morning. She couldn't sleep, she was so filled with excitement. She's going to call it "Lucy's Lighthouse" because her name means "bringer of light" and she wants to share the light of Jesus. She said, "Mom, we could film at gentleman's clubs and I could hand out Bibles, because that's what Jesus did!" I think that video might go viral, but it also might get Mommy arrested.

I love her spirit and I don't want to squash it. But I told her we had to pray about it because I know the battles of doing any kind of public ministry, and I'll do whatever I can to shield her from that kind of warfare. On the other hand, if she's following a call on her life from God, am I going to stop it? So I have to ask, "Is this a good idea? Or a God idea?" Because if something in your life is truly a "God idea," I believe there will be signs and confirmations. God will bless it with favor and you will see open doors. I'm not saying it will be easy, because the enemy hates God ideas. But when you are walking smack in the middle of God's will, whether you are 11 or 82, there is a peace to be had.

As I thought more about what Lucy wants to do, I decided to let her interview some of my friends who have public ministries and YouTube channels and even TV shows. Research is always a good idea and can help us make a wise decision instead of an emotional leap. Emotions and heart are incredible, but we need to partner them with the brain God gave us. And when we take time to ask God to be a part of our endeavors, He is more than happy to give us the best guidance we could ever ask for. It may be a great idea, but just not for such a time as this. And that's okay.

This subject reminds me of Solomon. When God told him he could have anything in the world, Solomon didn't ask for riches; he asked for wisdom. I'm not sure that's what I would have asked for if I had the same proposition from God. But I know it was the right answer, and God blessed him abundantly for it. So I'm off to do some praying, and we'll see what the future holds for my little future evangelist.

• • •

## TO THINK ON

- Can you think of a time you had a "good idea" and thought it was a "God idea…" but it turned out not to be?
- What would you do differently the next time you have an idea or an endeavor you want to pursue?

• • •

*Dear Lord,*

*Thank You for creating me with this brain that sometimes feels like it works a million miles a minute. I want all my actions to be in line with Your will for my life. Please remind me to slow down and talk to You before anyone else, because I know that should always be my first step.*

*In Jesus' name.*

*Amen.*

# THOUGHTS FROM A PROVERBS 32 MAN

*A wife of noble character who can find?*
*She is worth far more than rubies.*
*Her husband has full confidence in her*
*and lacks nothing of value.*
*She brings him good, not harm,*
*all the days of her life.*

**PROVERBS 31:10-12**

I've been doing a comedy tour for the last couple years with a comedian buddy Bob Smiley. It's called "Single Is Not a 4 Letter Word," and it's for Christian singles who want to laugh and have a night of inspiration. We always felt as though singles were sometimes a forgotten ministry in the church today so we put this tour together for them. It's been selling out all over the country, and it's a lot of fun. Just in case you need an update: I'm still dating Netflix!

Now, a lot of you have heard of Bob Smiley because he's famous; even my Lucy fangirled out when she found out I knew him! He rubbed that in my face for months. Bob recently ruined our tour by doing the unthinkable: he got married. I could kill him. But I'm thrilled he has settled down with an amazing wife. I'm still not sure how he got her. LOL! Here are some words of wisdom from a Proverbs 32 Man.

• • •

Proverbs 31 says an excellent wife is far more precious than jewels. That's ironic because a big jewel is usually involved in getting married. I know because I recently bought a wedding ring. I forgot to get the appraisal letter for insurance purposes, and when I went back to get it, the van was gone.

However, I finally found a Proverbs 31 wife! It took four years, but it was totally worth the search. My wife likes to point out that I didn't need to search as hard as I did, but that's beside the point. If you're looking for gold, you're probably going to see a lot of fool's gold along the way.

And actually, when I first became single again, I didn't even know where to look for a godly woman. My church's singles group consisted of me and Ms. Noosebalm. No offense to her, but I wasn't interested in dating someone who voted for Nixon.

Being forced back into the dating world made me wonder if there were any Proverbs 31 women still left on this tiny pebble called earth.

Fast-forward to two years into dating. I was discouraged and ready to give up. That's when God reminded me why He is God and I am not. I joke on stage that I met my wife on Myspace. We were the only two left, so it was easy!

The first thing I read about her was her love for Jesus. One phone call later...a six-hour phone call, to be exact...I knew this lady loved Jesus and would always love Jesus more than she loved me. She was the jewel I'd been promised in Proverbs.

I was used to aggressive females. If I swallowed my gum, they would offer to try to get it for me. Not this lady. She knew her worth and it showed. She didn't even kiss me until...well, we've been married for five months, so I'm sure it's going to happen soon.

Just a joke. However, Sarah takes comfort in knowing she is the daughter of the King. No man can replace the love that God has for her. And here's the good news: this is true for you as well. Once you realize how much God loves you, it sets you free to love others in a healthy way. She didn't have to settle. I had to earn her affection by being a godly man.

I watched Sarah love on her kids and mine. I watched her send encouraging notes to people going through a tough time. I watched and became a part of her amazing prayer life. In short, I found a diamond in the rough because she allowed God to guide her actions in every aspect of her life.

So that's my challenge to all the ladies reading this. Be a Proverbs 31 jewel and let us treasure hunters find you. Know your worth.

• • •

Hi, it's Kerri again. I agree with Bob that too often we are willing to take shortcuts just to get what we want. But is it what God has for us? Are we willing to hold on to the standards God set forth for us? If we really are a precious gem, don't we deserve to be treated like one?

• • •

## TO THINK ON

- Is there any area in your life where you've compromised your expectations and values just to get a quicker result?

- Do you see yourself as God's precious gem? Why or why not?

- How do you think God really sees you?

• • •

*Dear God,*

*Waiting is hard. Sometimes taking a shortcut seems like the path of least resistance. Please help me remember You are in control of my life.*

*Please help me remember that compromising my values is never a good decision and will only lead to heartache in the end.*

*In Jesus' name.*

*Amen.*

# GIVE AND TAKE A LITTLE

*Whoever knows the right thing to do
and fails to do it, for him it is sin.*

**JAMES 4:17 ESV**

have a great friend who is a fellow comedian named Lisa Mills. She is from the deep South, and even if she cursed you out it would sound sweet as pie. When you read this devotional, just picture Lisa's deep, southern drawl and appreciate this story about a wife who honors her husband, just like the Proverbs 31 Woman did.

• • •

My husband and I recently bought a house. We decided to remodel the property before moving in—you know, because that was easier than backing over each other with the car. (Seriously, the quickest route to divorce court is right through a Home Depot.) I'm not sure what made us think that tackling a remodel was something we should be doing. I mean, sure, my husband has contractor experience and is talented, but this has nothing to do with either of these facts. Tackling a remodel, or any huge project as a couple, is less about your skill and more about how you act as a team.

After more than two decades together, my husband and I know each other quite well. Actually, we have known each other since the seventh grade. And as a redheaded middle schooler with a perm and bad skin, let me say that any boy who has seen you at that stage of life and grows up to marry you is a hero, so this is in not a reflection of his commitment to me. I'm simply saying that there was no way we could have predicted how this remodel would test our level of hidden selfishness after being together for so long.

I detest selfishness, especially when I see it in myself. It's not something I struggle with normally, which is why I was very surprised that after arguing most of the evening over the color of light fixtures, I was determined to paint them the color I wanted after Richie left for work one morning. Goodbye, oil-rubbed bronze. Hello, high-gloss black! I wondered if he would notice they were different when he got home (or see and smell the paint I over-sprayed all over the garage floor).

Of course he noticed, but he said absolutely nothing. It wasn't until two days later that he casually mentioned the light fixtures and how good they looked. I was so proud of myself and was thinking I knew what looked better than he did when he said, "I've been thinking about the color you want to paint the front door and I'm not really set on that one." What? He knows I have wanted black shutters with a matching black door forever.

Marriage at its core is a series of days strung into decades of give and take. Nothing in a marriage will survive without really understanding this concept. Making mutual concessions, compromising regularly, and being willing to bend are keys to a healthy, long-lasting marriage. Ephesians 4:2-3 says, "Be completely humble and gentle; be patient, bearing with one another in love. Make every effort to keep the unity of the Spirit through the bond of peace." Unity isn't about agreement. If we think about it, unity doesn't even begin until agreement ends. When we can have ideas, thoughts, and feelings that are different from our spouse, and yet we can still be whole together—that is unity. Needless to say, our door is now dark gray, and I love it. Why? Because it made him happy. I got the lights, he got the front door, and that is marriage. Now, about those cabinets…

• • •

## TO THINK ON

- Can you think of a time when you compromised with another person and it paid off?

- Can you think of a time you were selfish and things did not go the way you planned? What could you have done differently?

• • •

*Dear Lord,*

*We are not naturally giving creatures. Please help me tame that inner voice that always wants things my way. Help me see others' views before jumping in to fight for my opinions. Help me to learn give and take.*

*In Jesus' name.*

*Amen.*

# FIRST-CLASS MIRACLE

*We know that in all things God works for the good of those*
*who love him, who have been called according to his purpose.*

**ROMANS 8:28**

It would be an understatement to tell you that my father has had some health challenges this past year. It's been one of the hardest years of our lives having to watch him suffer. We are no strangers to suffering, as we've each battled some major illnesses in our past, but this recent struggle has literally brought all of us to our knees. I love my dad so much. He is a cheerleader for me like no other. And by cheerleader, I also mean agent. He has been known to carry my headshot in his wallet to show people. I can't put into words how much it means to have him in my life. I've made a deal with God many times, begging Him to please not take my parents to heaven yet.

But this latest round of illness forced me to face the inevitable fact that someday I will not have my dad in my life. He's 79 years old, and much to my dismay, life on this earth is not eternal. I've cried so many tears of sadness, knowing how much my dad has been in pain and all the stress it's caused my mother as his caregiver, going from doctor to doctor for any hope of a solution. Today's modern medicine has come a long way, but there are many illnesses even the best doctors are scratching their heads over how to cure.

My dad has tried so many treatments and things have never gotten better. I just keep feeling led to pray to God these words: "I trust You. I know You have a plan to heal my dad." No matter how horrible things look, my mom and I continue to try to come up with a new treatment plan or facility that might help my dad get well. I know healing is going to have to be a supernatural God intervention.

A couple of weeks ago I sleepily rolled out of bed at the ripe hour of 5:00 a.m. and grabbed my bag to get to LAX to catch my flight to Florida. These early mornings aren't easy, but I had to take the time to look decent, because as my mother taught me, "Always dress nice to fly, because you never know who you're going to meet." This is wise advice, but I've yet to meet my internet millionaire, evangelist, musician single man yet. That's because I sit in coach. I only get to stare at the fancy folks as I head to my seats in steerage with the other peasants. There we snack on our pretzels while the people behind the curtain up front feast on crème brûlée and unlimited snacks.

Every once in a while I win the lottery and I get that ever-coveted first-class upgrade. Well, that morning I won! I was comfortably sipping my tea in seat 1-C, and a gentleman and I were enjoying our conversation. People are friendlier in first class. It must be the snacks.

We talked about our families and politics and whatever other topics came up to pass the time. At one point he mentioned something about struggling with a particular illness. I about dropped my chocolate mousse because it was the *exact* same thing my father was dealing with! But this man was mountain biking and fit as a fiddle. He told me his story about how hopeless he was until he discovered a specialist who got him on a new trial medication that literally cured him immediately. I listened intently, and he was kind enough to give me the drug name and even the name of his doctor.

I jetted off the plane when we landed (pardon the pun), called my mom, and told her the story. She had heard of this medication and had already looked into it but was told my dad didn't qualify for it. "Call again!" I said.

Mom's been a pit bull advocate for my dad so she took a chance. The doctor said it would be risky, but if my dad was willing to come in and be monitored for side effects and reactions, he would administer the treatment.

I talked to my dad the night before his treatment and he said, "Kerri, this is the first time I've felt some real hope. I know your prayers are working." My dad went the next day to try the new medication, and he felt better that same day. I was driving when I heard the news and tears fell from my eyes. I just kept saying, "Thank You, God! Thank You, God, for healing my dad!" He did have some side effects, but nothing that would stop him from continuing on with this path of treatment.

Overall, my dad is better today as I write this, but we know we have a long road ahead. We are not out of the woods by any means, and it's still so hard to see him in pain. But that medication did serve a purpose, and I am grateful that God knew where I'd be sitting on the airplane that day. God knew the plan He had for my dad, and every moment was under His umbrella of mercy.

When you have been walking through some tough or troubling circumstances, can you look back and see how God was moving behind the scenes? Was He placing you in just the right seat somewhere or just the right situation? It's hard to see God at work when we're in the thick of things. But it's always a good idea to take a look back and be grateful. These stories encourage others and show that we serve a very hands-on God who is never asleep behind the wheel. He is constantly watching us, guiding us, and sometimes even "upgrading" us when we least expect it. And let me just say that the chicken cordon bleu in first class was delicious!

* * *

## TO THINK ON

- Can you think of a time God was ordaining circumstances on your behalf and it was completely unplanned?

- Do you get impatient waiting for God to do something you've been praying for? How do you find patience?

* * *

*Dear God,*

*I don't even pretend to understand Your plans or Your timing. I can say with all seriousness that You are the master craftsman of our lives and circumstances. Help me remember You have a better view of my life than I do. Help me trust You at all times, even when I can't see the light.*

*In Jesus' name.*

*Amen.*

# GET OVER IT!

*As far as the east is from the west,*
*so far has he removed our transgressions from us.*

**PSALM 103:12**

So, I sinned. I know I know…shocking right?

But seriously, I did something I knew before, during, and after was wrong, and that knowledge did not stop me one bit. I was sort of surprised at myself because I'm a grown Christian woman and I knew better. But I suppose so did Eve when she ate the fruit, and so did David when he was looking at Bathsheba, and so did all the others we read about in the Bible. So yes, I took Satan's bait, and he didn't even have to work that hard this time. I own this one.

But now I have a problem that is rooted in the whack theology I've come up with for myself and no one else on the whole forgiveness concept. It's like I can preach forgiveness and our loving God's mercy night and day, but when it comes to me, I somehow feel the same rules don't apply. For example, last night before bed, when I so clearly knew I had done something wrong, I couldn't even bring myself to ask for forgiveness because that seemed too easy.

I prayed, "Dear God, yes, I know that was bad. I don't expect You to forget that happened. I know that sin has consequences and You said, 'The wages of sin is death' (Romans 6:23). But please don't kill me before I can wake up tomorrow morning and give You a proper guilt-infused apology, along with an entire day of questioning what kind of Christian I am. And when I'm done paying my penance (I grew up

Catholic), I will feel I am somewhat worthy of Your forgiveness. But I will still be watching my back for something bad to happen. I love You very much. Amen."

Some of you are judging my insanity. The rest of you Proverbs 32 women are saying to yourself, "How did she get into my head? I didn't even grow up Catholic!" I've given this some thought, and I believe we try to make God human with human qualities and emotions. A rational human being might not jump to forgive and forget someone who knowingly hurt them. But we're told that is exactly what God will do the minute we say we are sorry. However, it feels too much like a "get out of hell free" card concept to me. How can I royally mess up, hurt God, and then say sorry and just brush it off like it never happened?

I know I still have a lot to learn about forgiveness. After all, David wrote entire psalms about how his sin and guilt literally made him sick. God made us to have guilty feelings for a reason. I'm sure so we could realize that sin is painful to all parties involved. I could look at the fact that it bothers me that I did something displeasing to God as a good thing. I'm growing in my walk. I'm sensitive to the Holy Spirit, and I love God so much I don't want to think I've made Him sad.

It's funny that I struggle with this, because after I punish my kids for something they did wrong, they are good to go. They are not sulking around the house in anguish about their actions. They know Mommy always forgives them, and I even always say, "I never stop loving you, even when you disobey me." They choose to believe me, and because of our track record together, their belief holds true. God says it is good for us to be like children, and I definitely need to follow their example.

I think in times like this it would be a good idea to read in the Bible about all the times God's children turned their backs on Him, sinned against Him, and were really rotten. And how many times did God forgive them? Every single time. Even I was pretty annoyed at the Israelites in the Old Testament. God literally rescued them and saved their very lives over and over and over. Then Moses goes up that mountain for one minute and someone's building a golden calf. I'm not different, though. My golden calves are just a bit more private but no less sinful.

I'm glad I have a personal relationship with God on a day like today because I need Him to help me sort this out. I have a friend Gina whom I called this morning and told everything that happened. She reminded me of the truth about myself. I made a mistake. I repented before the Lord, and now I have to walk in freedom. If I don't do that, I'm actually denying what Jesus died for in the first place. I certainly don't want to add that to my "naughty list."

There is no statute of limitations of how long we have to wait before we can be forgiven. We humans made the idea that we have to do penance before we can accept God's forgiveness, and the enemy has been all too happy to help us reinforce that in our minds. So today I will clear my mind, pick myself up, and keep going. That's what I would want my kids to do, and that's what God wants His kids to do. Anything less is just silly.

• • •

## TO THINK ON

- Have you ever had trouble accepting God's grace and forgiveness for yourself?
- How did you handle your feelings?

• • •

*Dear God,*

*Your Word so clearly states that You died for my sins. Please help me take that statement literally and stop suffering with guilt and shame that You didn't want me to have to bear. Thank You for dying for my freedom and giving me the gift of second and third chances. I love You.*

*In Jesus' name.*

*Amen.*

# GOOD NEWS, BAD NEWS

*I have told you these things, so that in me you may have peace.*
*In this world you will have trouble.*
*But take heart! I have overcome the world.*

**JOHN 16:33**

Some people look at the glass half empty. Others see the glass half full. There are people like my mother who look at the glass and say, "Why are you using these glasses? They are plastic!" (Love you, Mom!)

Over the last 24 hours I've gotten some really good news. My mom's doctor declared she's eight years cancer-free. I prayed for one of my mom's friends who was in serious pain from sciatica and all her pain went away. I woke up without back pain ready to go work out again after taking a month off from a back injury. I turned in a writing project, and my lovely editor sent me the sweetest note that she loved it. I have a conference call with a TV network today about a movie they want me to write. I measured my daughter Ruby's growth yesterday morning and she has grown! So why do I feel so melancholic?

Well, along with my mom's great cancer news, her doctor thought he heard a heart irregularity, and though the EKG was normal, we were stressed with worry until she got the results. My dad is very sick this morning. The woman who has the sciatica pain is also dealing with stage 4 cancer. And I got on the scale for the first time in over a month and the number was shockingly high. I might get kicked out of LA. As I was getting ready for my day I got a debilitating migraine headache.

And at my daughter's yearly physical the doctor said she hadn't grown enough and wants her to see a specialist.

So life to me feels much like a seesaw, and I'm always trying to find the perfect balance so I don't crash down and get hurt. When we were kids and played on the seesaw for hours, there was never a power struggle to see who was carrying the most weight. No matter who was on it, we made it work and enjoyed the ride. The only problem was when one person decided to unexpectedly get off and the other person went down in a huge *thud*.

As I sit here pondering all the things listed above, it occurs to me that this yin-yang is the human existence. In heaven there will be no bad news or suffering, but while we are down here we face an enemy whose daily pursuit is to steal our joy. If he can make Christians negative-thinking, hopeless, and sullen, he wins. He knows we will not attract anyone over to our belief in Christ if our lives are full of sadness, defeat, and hopelessness.

We can choose to look at all of our situations in life like a seesaw. We need the good and the bad to balance each other. If our lives were perfect, why would we need a Savior? But God is always on the move and always sending us moments of good news as encouragement to keep going. And when we feel like we're stuck on the ground, we can remember God is always on the other side of the seesaw, ready to bring us back up.

God is our balancing partner. I know as soon as I win any battle, the enemy is going to throw another one my way. Jesus told us this exact thing was going to happen and that we should expect trials. But He told us He overcame the world, and so could we. When my mom called me about my dad being sick today, I reminded her that God healed her cancer and kept it away for eight years. And if God can heal my mom's cancer, He can heal my dad and her friend. And if God healed Ruby of all those incurable diseases at birth (which He did), He can make her taller. And if the TV thing doesn't work out, my editor thinks I'm a great writer.

I hear sermons preached about how God wants us to live the fullest, best life possible. People sometimes take that to mean we'll be rich, skinny, and never have any troubles. But I think what God wants is for me to put my hope in Him. There is no problem He can't handle, no obstacle He can't help me face, and no prayer request too big. He sent His Son to die for us so we could put our armor on daily and overcome the enemy's schemes.

I pray that prayer daily with my kids, and I have to know the battle is mostly in my mind. How am I going to look at every situation? I will not focus on the problem. I will focus on the provider of my solution. Now, if the Lord could remove the enemy's carefully placed chocolate chip cookies from my pantry so I won't eat them at 1:00 a.m., I would be so grateful!

• • •

## TO THINK ON

- Are you a glass half empty or half full person?
- When you are faced with a problem or bad news, can you find a way to balance it with something good God is doing within the situation?

• • •

*Dear God,*

*Thank You for knowing the good news. I need to keep running this race we call life. I love You and trust that You are the only One who can take away my sadness. Please remind me that it is not Your will for me to be imbalanced and that You are always right there on the seesaw with me.*

*In Jesus' name.*

*Amen.*

# RIDING THE CRAZY TRAIN

*The one who gets wisdom loves life...*

**PROVERBS 19:8**

W hen I was first starting out in comedy there was a wonderful lady named Pam who was very encouraging to me. I later came to know her as a very gifted and successful author. Pam is a cheerleader to so many people, and I am honored she decided to share a story for this devotional. I know you will enjoy it.

. . .

I was born on the wrong side of the tracks. My parents met while doing migrant farm labor in Oregon. My mom came to stay with relatives the summer after her high school graduation and fell in love, and she stayed in this tiny town where the lumberyard and the railroad tracks were in my front yard.

My creative, loving mom kept us kids fooled about just how broke we were. At the end of the month, when Mother Hubbard looked in her cupboard and found it was almost bare, she tore up stale, hard, old Wonder Bread, put the pieces in brightly colored tin cups, and poured in the last of the milk. Then she tucked us in bed, reading a borrowed Golden Book. My mom tried her best to turn bad into good.

Yet there were still those railroad tracks marking our lack of social status in our little town. Those tracks would become symbolic of the Crazy Train our family would ride for decades.

Our tickets were punched for the Crazy Train when my mom

married in rebellion to her parents' wishes. My father, who started out the good-hearted, fun, kind, life-of-the-party, beer in one hand, cigarette in the other guy, would soon evolve into the chief engineer of the Crazy Train. Born the middle child of ten on a dirt farm during the *Grapes of Wrath* depression days, my daddy had a well-earned red neck from hard labor under the hot sun. He and his brothers had to quit school to help provide for the family because their daddy spent every day going to the "office" (the tavern).

My dad began drinking and smoking very early in life. Beer is the sap of my family tree. And all that drinking soon turned my happy-go-lucky father into a depressed, angry, and often violent man. The chief of police of our hamlet lived down the street, and he was our personal 911.

Miraculously, because my dad had some brilliant DNA, he eventually got a job as a car mechanic. One day a rep from a farm machinery company came through town and recognized my father's talent for fixing things and offered him a job with a real salary, benefits, and a company car. Dad, for a time, was happy, but the thing about riding a Crazy Train is it becomes a habit, and the dysfunctions of one generation pass to the next *unless* heaven intervenes.

As a kindergartener, I would get up early and sit in front of our hand-me-down, black-and-white TV on Sunday mornings. I would watch a cartoon that shared Bible stories, and a show with a dad who was a loving, wise, kind, and godly Christian man. I began to talk to a God I knew was there but no one had introduced me to. "That's the kind of family I want," I would pray.

That year my folks had the kind of knock-down, drag-out argument that makes for small town gossip. My mom's best friend, Kathy, the secretary of the small Christian church, saw the chaos we were living in, invited my mom to church, and told her to bring us kids. That Sunday I knew I wanted to know the God of love these folks worshiped. I was sure I wanted to go to heaven one day, especially if God handed out graham crackers with frosting and red punch.

If you memorized a verse in Sunday school, they let you choose a prize, so when I memorized Psalm 23 with the promise that "surely your goodness and love will follow me all my life," I drew out a cross that glowed in the dark. I proudly pinned it to my closet in my bedroom.

One night I was memorizing Matthew 5–7 so I could have a place on Quiz Team (in our small town that was like appearing on *American Idol*!) I came across Matthew 7:7: "Ask and it will be given to you; seek and you will find; knock and the door will be opened to you." Just then my daddy, who had been drinking all day and night, went into a fit of anger, so I ran to get my little brother and sister and took them to my room and pushed the dresser in front of the door so Dad couldn't get in to hurt us. I tucked them in bed, turned off the light, and climbed in too.

There, glowing in the dark, was that little cross and it read, "Jesus Lives." I prayed, "Lord, when I grow up, I don't want to have a home like this, all out of control and crazy. I want a home like Kathy's, who brought us to a church that is full of love, joy, peace, and patience. So please come into my life. And P.S., when I grow up, I would like to marry a pastor one day."

That's the day I learned I didn't have to ride that Crazy Train. I had choices. And that decision to welcome Jesus into my life led me through a series of better choices that eventually led me to a college Christian conference where I met a curly-headed, tan, cool California boy, whose mother, like my dad, was a daily commuter on the Crazy Train. And this boy wanted to be a pastor!

We consider our love, and 40-year happy marriage, a miracle. Our family became a miracle too. My mother, siblings, and eventually even my daddy decided to surrender to Jesus' love. Bill and I, and our grown children, now help others get off the Crazy Train!

• • •

## TO THINK ON

- What is a dysfunction in your family of origin that you want to replace with something healthier?

- Is there a habit in your life that keeps putting you back on the Crazy Train?

- Is there a person you can talk to for help? Or is there a verse you can pin on your closet door that would give you hope for your future?

• • •

*Dear God,*

*I don't want to live in a state of craziness, chaos, and confusion. Please show me what to release to You, and what verses about You to focus on to get off and stay off the Crazy Train.*

*In Jesus' name.*

*Amen.*

# SECOND HALF COMEBACK

*Nothing will be impossible with God.*

**LUKE 1:37 NASB**

love a good comeback story. Even if it's cheesy fiction, if the main character was down for the count and then that music starts to play (you know, when it pounds slowly at first and then getting faster and louder…think *Rocky*) and you know our hero is going to come back from defeat and be better than ever, I'm going to cry. I also love a good sporting event when my team is down at the half and comes back in the second quarter and pounces on the opponents for the big win. #GOBLUE

Our lives are a series of comebacks. Sometimes you've been knocked down so many times by the devil, you don't even see that there is a whole second half of your life ahead of you. The devil's job is to get you down and keep you there, because if you feel unsuccessful you may not walk into that comeback destiny God has planned for you.

There are plenty of stories about people who had one big setback and then overcame the odds. Michael Jordan didn't make his high school basketball team, for example. But what about those of you who feel your life is at a complete standstill and you know there is something more out there for you but you don't know how to begin to reach for it. You may have been kicked down so hard and so many times you forgot how to rise up out of the ashes.

You might think these amazing second-half stories are for Hollywood movies, not regular people. I beg to differ. My dad never had a musical lesson in his life. But at the age of 62, he took out a pen and paper and a tape recorder and wrote country songs and lyrics. He can't play piano, he can't read music, and many might say he was well beyond the appropriate age to be a professional writer. He had no special connections either. But he sang these songs into his recorder and then found some local artists who were willing to demo record his songs.

One song he wrote for my mom, who served in Vietnam, was called "We Cry Together at the Wall." It was a tribute to vets. My dad had some demo CDs made and sent them around to music people and someone heard that song. Long story short, the people who represent the Vietnam Memorial Wall asked if they could use my dad's song when they do memorial events all around the world. And he got two more of his songs on the International Country Music charts. How's that for a second half? He's 79 years old today, and his songs have been heard all over the world.

One day when my mom was in her sixties, she decided she would take those letters she wrote my dad from Vietnam and turn them into a memoir, *Seas of War*, for her children. She was a Red Cross worker who helped the wounded on a hospital ship called USS *Repose*. Well, wouldn't you know, she self-published that book, and soldiers my mom had taken care of actually read the book and were able to find my mom and thank her. She now speaks for veteran organizations, and her book is in its third printing. Today she's 75! My mom has had 25 surgeries and cancer three times. The devil was trying to keep a good woman down, but today she is cancer-free and her story is read all over the world.

Don't ever let anyone tell you that you don't have a second half in you. Maybe you have a dream you thought was dead. Who's to say God's not just waiting for you to take the first step? Do you have a book inside you? Do you know how I published my first book? I took my *real* diaries from third grade onward and started transcribing them into a Word document. It took me four years to finish it, but my story got picked up by a publisher and is still in circulation today and has even been translated into different languages.

God is a God of the comeback. Just look at the heroes in the Bible and their second halves. David could have gone to jail for murder; instead, he became the most beloved king of his generation. Abraham and Sarah thought God was done with them, and yet He gave them Isaac in the later years of their lives, who was in the genealogy line of Jesus. And what about Job? He had every reason to throw in the towel on life itself and no one would have blamed him. But the Bible says his later days were more blessed than the first.

I know one thing for sure: God is not done with you. He's just getting started. God might be opening doors for you, but you need to make the choice to walk through them. Don't believe the lies about yourself. He created you for greatness. The first step is to believe it!

• • •

## TO THINK ON

- Are you at a standstill in any area of your life? What is it? Why?

- Do you believe God could have a comeback in store for you? What could it be?

• • •

*Dear Lord,*

*Help me dream with You and restore my hope for better days. Help me get back up and put myself in the game again even when it looks impossible. You are the author of my story and I believe it is good.*

*In Jesus' name.*

*Amen.*

# Day 60

# GRACE

Kerri@proverbs32woman.com

My dearest Kerri,

Well, you did it again. You made me laugh so loudly I believe all of heaven must have heard me. I was quite pleased to hear from you again. I hope you don't mind, but I shared your first book with some of my friends. Martha said to tell you, "Thanks for the shout-out." She said she was going to write you a note, but right now she's preparing some rooms in the many mansions and she's quite busy.

I can see very clearly that although you've been hurt, you haven't lost your hope for love in your life. And it seems you are learning the very important lesson that whether you are wearing a ring on your finger or not, the most intimate relationship you will ever have is with your Lord and Savior. He is always faithful and will never let you down. You can trust Him with your deepest secrets, your innermost fears, and your greatest desires. He is the truest love you will ever find.

I wish more women could grasp the wholeness of this truth sooner rather than later while they are on earth. It seems to me they spend more time believing the lies of the world about themselves than the truths that were so clearly expressed for them in God's holy Word. There are so many love letters from God to us in His Word and so many examples of His undying love for His daughters.

It is incomprehensible the amount of sheer joy and utter bliss I felt the moment I got to experience God's love here in heaven. I can't say too much; I want you to be surprised.

But having a book like this sure might come in handy for women on earth, with all the hustle and bustle of their daily lives. I don't know how you manage it all. You think we had it hard? Your generation is overwhelmed with every distraction you can imagine pulling you away from having a relationship with your Savior. I might have thought it was easier for you ladies to get in the Word because you can find it in all forms, even on those screens of yours. But it seems so overwhelming to me with so many choices. Back in my day, hearing from God started on two stone tablets. And you heard how that turned out!

So I consider your recent effort a valuable resource for women from all walks of life. I pray they use it wisely. And I admire your candor and vulnerability. It certainly will let women know they are not the most mixed-up gal in the world. Am I right? Ha-ha! See? You're not the only funny one, my dear. If they learn one thing from all of your stories, I hope it will be just how much they are truly, madly, and passionately loved by God. And that will never change.

Well, my friend, I must be going. Until we meet again. I look forward to hearing from you.

Yours,
Grace (Proverbs 31 Woman)

P.S. I think there is a phone up here; try this number if you get a chance.

867-5309

## Note to Reader

I hope you have enjoyed this devotional and it's given you some new perspectives on God's grace, love, and maybe even sense of humor. If you have your own Proverbs 32 Woman stories, I want to hear them. Do you eat cereal for dinner? Stockpile paper plates? Please check out our Facebook page, Proverbs 32 Woman, or email me at Kerri@proverbs32woman.com. We're starting the movement of Nutella-eating, Netflix-watching, crazy-about-God Proverbs 32 women! Join the revolution!

## Acknowledgments

Thank You to God for delivering me from every evil that I tried to get myself into all these years that made for great stories.

I want to thank my super-editor, Kathleen Kerr, for helping this devotional become a real grown-up book.

Thank you to Tricia Heyner and Pam Couzin for inspiring me to use punctuation.

Thank you to Debbie and Renee, who read all my crazy stories and cried so I knew they were good.

Thank you to Greg Johnson, my super-agent, who always tells me I'm a good writer and that I'm pretty.

Thank you to the Harvest House team for their unending kindness.

Thank you to my parents and family who inspire these stories daily—especially Lucy and Ruby, who just open their mouths and I write it down and take all the credit.

Thank you to Bob, Lisa, Claire, and Pam, who made this book extra special.

Thank you to my many prayer warriors out there who fight behind the scenes for me doing this "Christian thing" in Hollywood.

And thank you to Marlo Blanford and Laurie Short for inviting me to coffee that day!

## About the Author

**Kerri Pomarolli** lives by the sea but never goes in it. She has two daughters and has appeared on many TV shows, including *The Tonight Show*, shows on Comedy Central, and many more. She's usually traveling the country doing clean comedy or speaking at ministry events. She is a screen writer for the Hallmark Channel and spends an inappropriate amount of time on social media. You can find her on Instagram @kerripom or www.kerripom.com. Write her. She needs attention.

# CONFESSIONS OF A
# PROVERBS 32 WOMAN

*How I Went from Messed Up to Blessed Up*
*Without Changing a Single Thing*

## KERRI POMAROLLI

## GOD IS CRAZY ABOUT YOU— HOT MESS AND ALL!

If you're anything like Kerri Pomarolli, you've read Proverbs 31 and thought, "Who is this woman? And what kind of magic unicorn, Energizer Bunny juice does she have on IV?"

And you thought social media standards were hard to live up to!

As a sought-after comedian living in LA, Kerri knows about impossible standards. "I don't plow, and I don't rise early. When it says she gathers her food from afar, does that mean takeout…?"

In *Confessions of a Proverbs 32 Woman,* Kerri fearlessly shares the messiness of her own life with wit and honesty. Join her as she delves into the struggles of the modern woman tired of trying and failing to live up to Pinterest-looking, air-brushed, and insta-filtered "real life" role models telling her she's not *quite* good enough. And learn the two things you can hold onto for longer than your smartphone: genuine self-awareness and humble God-awareness.

Kerri is a self-proclaimed hot mess for Jesus who has learned that God never said our lives would be mess-less, but He also never intended for us to wallow forever without a way through. When you're at your most hopeless, God and His Word will meet you in there, where you'll find, as Kerri has, that this #hotmess4Jesus thing really can be the best possible life to live.

# BOOKING INFORMATION

**Kerri Pomarolli** has been performing in churches, at retreats, and for outreach events for more than 12 years to sellout crowds. She's known as Hollywood's Favorite God Girl and isn't afraid to stand up for her faith. In addition to *The Tonight Show* and *Comedy Central,* she's appeared on ABC, TBN, NBC, and many more.

She's hosted at the Gospel Music Awards and worked with Jim Carey, Jay Leno, Pat Boone, The Jonas Brothers, Joni Eareckson Tada, Tim Hawkins, and Candace Cameron Bure, to name a few. She's a gifted event MC and has been on stage for many causes, such as the Hollywood Abstinence Coalition, Heart for Africa, and Pregnancy Resource Centers nationwide. Kerri is the kind of Christian everyone can relate to no matter what their background. From ages 8 to 80, audiences will fall in love with her clean comedy and come back for more.

She's the perfect choice for your next

- fundraiser
- singles group
- women's event
- family outreach
- retreat
- Sunday morning service

Not only does she provide hilarious comedy, she's a gifted inspirational speaker who shares the gospel in an approachable way. She's also highly requested for keynotes at corporate events. If you want lots of laughs and impactful content, you want Kerri Pomarolli.

Booking info at booking@kerripom.com
www.kerripom.com
Instagram @kerripom
Facebook / Twitter / YouTube: Kerri Pomarolli

"Blown Away!" The only words I can use to describe the "Night with Kerri." Kerri Pomarolli blew our church away with her hilarious and uplifting stories and antics…The combination of her comedy and vulnerable ministry was a win for all our families. She stayed well into the evening praying and interacting with each person. We've already invited her back again.

Blake N. Sitz, senior pastor, The Well Gadsden, Gadsden, Alabama

To learn more about Harvest House books and
to read sample chapters, visit our website:

**www.harvesthousepublishers.com**

**HARVEST HOUSE PUBLISHERS**
EUGENE, OREGON